T0355175

Winner of Honorable Mention from the Modernist Studies Association

Praise for *Second Skin*

"Anne Cheng deftly examines how Josephine Baker became a discursive fetish for Modernism, handled by architects, directors, photographers, writers, and many, many others. By training her gaze not on race but on skin, Cheng shows what Baker revealed about her times rather than what Baker's times revealed about her. In both the annihilating and rejuvenating senses, this book skins Modernism alive."

—**Kenji Yoshino**, author of *Covering:
The Hidden Assault on Our Civil Rights*

"Cheng's analysis of the relationships between Josephine Baker's artful self-exposure and Modernist architecture's insistence on pure surface is marvelously inventive!"

—**Coco Fusco**, author of *The Bodies That Were Not Ours*

"For a long time now, Frantz Fanon's *Black Skin, White Masks* has been the primary text through which many of us have conceptualized race. Anne Cheng's *Second Skin* offers a compellingly different account of race. Like the story recounted by Fanon, Cheng's is about seeing and being seen, but hers takes place in the first half of the twentieth century and revolves around a female body whose shining surface repels, rather than instantiates, every attempt to assign it a color, or equip it with a psychic or corporeal interiority."

—**Kaja Silverman**, author of *Flesh of My Flesh*

"This brilliant, provocative, eye-opening work provides a powerful account of racial fetishism and its centrality to the development of Modernist style, thus forwarding a stunning new theory of Modernism in its entirety."

—**Sianne Ngai**, author of *Ugly Feelings*

"Anne Cheng's *Second Skin* offers an innovative, surprising, deeply transdisciplinary archaeology of aesthetic Modernism's relationship to race and its performances. Le Corbusier, Adolf Loos, Picasso, Paul Valéry, and Freud's psychoanalysis become partners in this dizzying theoretical and historical analysis, where Cheng reveals how buildings, fashion, photographs, paintings, and dances express as well as construct our shared legacy of racial formations."

—**André Lepecki**, author of *Exhausting Dance: Performance and the Politics of Movement*

"In a bravura meditation on the surfaces at the core of Modernism—skin, costume, canvas, screen, ornament, pattern—Anne Anlin Cheng tracks the vicissitudes of visual pleasure in the encounter between Europe and its others. *La Baker* was not simply a lightning rod for exotic stereotypes, Cheng suggests, but instead a 'dynamic fulcrum' whose performances captivated because they staged the crosscurrents that define Modernist style, its dangerous intimacies between primitive and civilized, animal and machine, organic and plastic."

—**Brent Hayes Edwards**, author of *The Practice of Diaspora*

"Opening up an entirely original line of inquiry that connects the architectural surfaces of Adolf Loos and Le Corbusier to the shimmering allure of Josephine Baker's skin, this far-reaching study gives us a unique model of cross-cultural modernity in which psychoanalysis has a major role to play. With wit, verve, and precision, Anne Cheng's insights ensure that our understanding of early Modernism will never be the same and that our notions of phantasy and identification in art, film, and performance will be radically transformed."

—**Kobena Mercer**, author of *Welcome to the Jungle*

"Through a series of deft readings of the archival traces of Baker's early performances . . . Cheng effectively illustrates how Baker wielded skin as kind of sheath, turning disrobing, paradoxically, into an act of concealment and troubling structural binaries like surface/depth, exterior/interior, subject/object, and primitive/modern. . . . [I]n the context of white-dominated modernist culture, Baker's particular way of manifesting a 'modern surface' would seem to pose a historical question of valuation. Cheng's superb book takes us right to the edge of this crucial question: the question of how, why, and at what costs, the body of an African American woman becomes exchangeable as a commodity within a particular artistic and commercial context—or even becomes, reflexively, a symbol of this form of exchangeability within the money economy."

—*Historical Journal of Film, Radio and Television*

"A playful, insanely ambitious text that seeks to rethink standard assumptions about Modernism, race and Josephine Baker. . . . The book performs the admirable service of making Josephine Baker, the world she inhabited, and the skin that inhabited her, seem stranger and more complex than they did before."

—*cinespect.com*

Second Skin

Second Skin

Josephine Baker and the Modern Surface

Second edition

ANNE ANLIN CHENG

OXFORD
UNIVERSITY PRESS

Oxford University Press is a department of the University of Oxford. It furthers
the University's objective of excellence in research, scholarship, and education
by publishing worldwide. Oxford is a registered trade mark of Oxford University
Press in the UK and certain other countries.

Published in the United States of America by Oxford University Press
198 Madison Avenue, New York, NY 10016, United States of America.

Library of Congress Cataloging-in-Publication Data
Names: Cheng, Anne Anlin, author.
Title: Second skin : Josephine Baker and the modern surface / Anne Anlin Cheng.
Description: [2] edition. | New York, NY : Oxford University Press, [2023] |
Includes bibliographical references and index.
Identifiers: LCCN 2023032616 (print) | LCCN 2023032617 (ebook) |
ISBN 9780197748381 (hardback) | ISBN 9780197748404 (epub)
Subjects: LCSH: Modernism (Art) | Surfaces (Philosophy) | Arts, Modern—20th century. |
Arts and society—History—20th century. |
Baker, Josephine, 1906–1975—Criticism and interpretation.
Classification: LCC NX456.5.M64 C49 2023 (print) | LCC NX456.5.M64 (ebook) |
DDC 700/.4112—dc23/eng/20230802
LC record available at https://lccn.loc.gov/2023032616
LC ebook record available at https://lccn.loc.gov/2023032617

DOI: 10.1093/oso/9780197748381.001.0001

Printed by Sheridan Books, Inc., United States of America

To George IV, Anlin, and George V

We speak of [the body] to others as of a thing that belongs to us; but for us it is not entirely a thing; and it belongs to us a little less than we belong to it.

—Paul Valéry

Contents

Preface to the Second Edition

How do you escape voyeurism when *being seen* is your way out?

In the last twelve years since the initial publication of *Second Skin: Josephine Baker and the Modern Surface* (2011), specters of Baker continue to erupt in popular culture and capture the public imagination. In the last decade alone, a Prada collection cited Baker's famed banana skirt; Google released an animated doodle of Baker; and contemporary celebrities from Rihanna to Zendaya to Yara Shahidi to Miss France Clémence Botino continued to reenact Baker's feathers and bananas.

One either adores Baker or is embarrassed by her, sometimes both. To this day, in spite of all the sophisticated critiques of essentialism and identity politics, we still seem to require that our racial representatives remain redemptive, virtuous, uncomplicated. People want to canonize the Baker who helped the French Resistance but not so much the half-naked Baker in the *danse sauvage*. And if they do celebrate the latter, the citation always veers dangerously close to re-fetishization.

In 2021, Baker was inducted into the Panthéon, only the sixth woman and the first Black woman to receive such an honor. The news generated as much mockery as it did approbation in the French social media. One caricature that was trending on social media pictured Baker as a giantess climbing bare-bottomed out of the cupola of a miniaturized Panthéon. Whether you read this image as a racist and misogynist statement about Baker sullying the hallowed halls of the Panthéon or as a sly comment on Baker triumphantly riding the white masculine bastion that is the French mausoleum, it is clear that receptions of Baker continue to reproduce an unproductive, circular discourse of scorn and idealization. Baker remains to this day the most public and vivid example of a Black woman who is at once overexposed and suffering from narrative paucity. We keep telling the same stories about her.

Second Skin tells a different story about Baker. In writing this book, I was driven by my own startling encounter with the distinctiveness of Baker's theatrical strategy and style. Few have attended to the peculiar and strategic ways in which she deployed her body, visibility, movement, and costumes. How is it that no one noticed how her artistic oeuvres defy and, at times, even contradict all the well-known terms about her? Many, for example, allude to how Baker draws from the "African" and the "animal," but few have observed her affinity for the modern, the machine, and the abstract. Many speak of Baker's nakedness, yet few note her proclivity for covers and the covert.

What if, rather than rehearsing how great white modernists saw Baker, we were to ask, instead, how Baker has shaped, altered, and jeopardized some of the most deeply held beliefs and conceptual inventions of modernism itself?

Second Skin remains the first and only sustained monograph on the relationship between the theatricalization of Black skin at the turn of the twentieth century and the development of modern architectural theory. It is also a retelling of the origin stories of the white male masters (Adolf Loos, Le Corbusier, Pablo Picasso) credited for engineering modernism's conceptual and aesthetic revolutions. Viewing their innovations through the theoretical and reflective lens of Baker's art, and not the other way around, radically changes how we understand a host of foundational modernist preoccupations and their (disavowed) relationship to Blackness: notions such as the *denuded modern surface, transparency,* and *abstraction,* as well as a host of related ideas centering around the notion of a newly found, new-century *freedom.*

Rereading *Second Skin,* I continue to feel the urgency behind why I wrote this book: the need to think beyond the stubborn and killing limits of racial representation and what that says about the blind walls of our racial politics, especially dire in our increasingly racially divided world. *Second Skin* treats Baker as cipher, artist, and conceptual thinker. This is an account of how Baker, through intent and chance, shaped and altered the vocabulary of modern aesthetic theory. This entanglement between modern aesthetic theory and racialized gender, in turn, has much to teach us about a network of meanings and values that undergirds twentieth-century ideas of humanity and its others. Through close readings of her performance method in films, in photographs, and on the stage, I have come to see Baker as complicated and vexed, bold and sly, rebellious and compliant.

Baker was as much as vanishing artist as she was a canny exhibitionist. Her well-rehearsed iconography, often reduced to bare outlines or stranded synecdoches like a banana belt, has long blinded us to the fraught and endlessly engrossing ways in which her body of work activates what I've come to think of as her elaborate *sartorial epidermal schema*. This "skin play" on Baker's part plays a critically formative role in the making of the "clean minimalism" of high modern style. It also holds important lessons for us today for how we understand the terms of racial legibility and embodiment that continue to haunt feminism, race studies, and their embroilment with aesthetic theory. It was in writing this book that I realized that I was working toward a larger meditation on an alternative logic of racial modality, one that is not dependent on the flesh or even the organic, even if it likes to speak in the language of corporeality and desire, an idea that I went on to develop more extensively in the study *Ornamentalism*.

This volume digs deeply, intellectually, and conceptually into Baker as performer and artist without ever forgetting that agency and authorship are fraught and fragile things for an African American woman making her way in a white world in the 1920s and '30s.

How do you escape voyeurism when being seen is your way out? You disappear into the visible.

For Baker, ostentatious display *was* her fugitivity.

This is my story about the mysteries of the visible.

Anne Anlin Cheng
January 2023

Acknowledgments

Writing this book brought together many loves and several origins. I must begin by thanking the haunting of Josephine Baker. I hope this project captures in some measure her mercurial spirit. This book came into focus and was completed here at Princeton, which holds special meanings for me: many years ago, Sam Hunter allowed an undergraduate into his graduate seminar, threw her in the deep end with expectations tempered by generosity, and instilled in her an abiding love for modern art and architecture. It was also here, in a memorable course taught by P. Adams Sitney, that I first experienced the profound pleasures of reading film. In the years since, I have taken many different paths, but working on Baker allowed me to dwell in these passions, for which I am grateful.

Anyone who has undertaken an interdisciplinary project knows how much collaboration it takes. The Townsend Center Strategic Working Group on "When Is Art Research?" at the University of California, Berkeley, and the "Engendering Archive" Working Group at Columbia University provided me with important interlocutors at the beginning and near the end of this project. I am grateful to the wisdom of Amelie Hastie at *Camera Obscura*, Elizabeth Weed at *differences*, Kimberlyn Leary at *Psychoanalytic Quarterly*, and Stephen Best and Sharon Marcus at *Representations*, who published articles that were working toward this larger project and whose comments helped me think through issues beyond those essays. I thank my editors at Oxford University Press: Shannon McLachlan for her vision and faith in this book; Brendan O'Neill and Tamzen Benfield for being so good at what they do, and Hannah Doyle who has fast become a valued ally. Michelle Coghlan, Jessica Davis, and Tao Leigh Goffe not only gave me invaluable research assistance, but they also honored me with their friendships. This book is indebted to the kindness of strangers as well: to Leo Lensing for sharing his knowledge of Vienna at the turn of the century and to Farès el-Dahdah for generously sharing his digital recreation of the Josephine Baker House.

Conversations with the following amazing individuals, either about or outside of work, invariably lift the fog or take me to imaginative new places: Gregory Blatman, Daphne Brooks, Eduardo Cadava, Raveevarn Choksombatchai, Beatrice Colomina, Jill Dolan, Diana Fuss, Claudia Johnson, Jeff Nunakawa, Valerie Smith, Michael Wood, and, as ever, Valentina Vavasis. And because a book is also a space of memory, I wish to remember Barbara Johnson, whose work always opened up windows that end up readjusting vision itself; and the late William Nestrick, who gave me support in ways that to this day I suspect I am not even fully aware of.

Several friends read sections of the manuscript and, in some cases, the entire manuscript. I thank them for their generosity and for their exquisitely idiosyncratic minds. Jason Friedman kept me going with our fascination for Baker and with his steadfast friendship. Robert Hass helped me stay close to what touches the heart. Susan Stewart unstintingly shared her insights along with her warmth and good humor. My dear friends Sarah Deyong, Spyridon Papapetros, and Sarah Whiting guided me through the world of architectural theory. I treasure my vision of the lovely Sharon Marcus reading my manuscript in a café in Paris and am thankful for the kind of comments that only she can make. It was Saidiya Hartman who first showed me that I was writing a book about Baker before I was even prepared to acknowledge it to myself. She gave me the courage to undertake this book. Her good counsel, on matters small and large, continues to sustain me in the life of the mind and just plain life.

The course of this project saw the passing of my father, who gave me much of who I am today and who modeled the importance of a life worth living. My mother, who is ten times stronger than she thinks, inspires (even shames) me with her grace and courage. Finally, this book is dedicated to my children, Anlin and George, my most cherished distractions and beloved anchors; and to my husband, George R. Kopf, who always makes me feel at home in my own skin even as his superhuman strength makes it possible—and exhilarating—for me to venture beyond the comfortable. He, very simply, brought meaning.

1

Her Own Skin

Why should modern architects who abhor ornamentation, tattoos, and other erotic markings choose to think about the surfaces of their buildings as "skins"? Why do the first modern bathing suits bear a graphic resemblance to nineteenth-century prison uniforms? What do museum displays have to do with burlesque performances? Is the twentieth-century fascination for transparency a pleasure about seeing *into* or *through* things?

This book turns our attention to the mysteries of the visible and how those mysteries dwell on the surfaces that we think we know all too well. The above, seemingly unrelated questions of style—and really of desire—are all part of what I call modernism's dream of a second skin. And our entry into this story will be the surprising figure of Josephine Baker, a woman who achieves international fame overnight for wearing her nakedness like a sheath (figure 1.1).

With three memoirs, more than twenty biographies in English and French, and a wealth of images preserved and replicated, Baker's story appears to be as well excavated as her nudity was widely publicized. One has only to invoke her name (no, even just hint at the barest gestural outline of her figure) and all that she stands for—the racist and sexist history of objectification and of desire that makes up the phenomenon of European primitivism or, conversely, the idealization of Black female agency—immediately materializes. Yet what would it mean to see Baker not as an example of but as a fracture in the representational history of the Black female body? Why is it unimaginable to reflect on the ways in which her performance style—even her body type—might not fit into established tropes such as the Venus Hottentot? Although the history of racialized femininity would seem to insist on a relentless story about the coercions of the visible, we might want to ask, how is it we know we are seeing what we think we are seeing? What are the conditions under which we see?

Second Skin. Second edition. Anne Anlin Cheng, Oxford University Press. © Oxford University Press 2023.
DOI: 10.1093/oso/9780197748381.003.0001

Fig. 1.1
On or about December, 1910, human character changed.
—*Virginia Woolf*

The givenness of Baker's race and gender and what those categories
mean for a European audience at the turn of the twentieth century has
led almost all critics of Baker to position her in a well-established tradition of colonial Black female representation. For a large segment of

feminist critics, Baker indubitably and specifically references the figure of the Venus Hottentot.[1] This critical certitude, however, has unwittingly limited the context in which we can consider Baker. One *sympathetic* critic goes as far as to suggest that there is not much there to be studied: "Looking at Josephine . . . —that endearing but not-precisely-pretty face, the honey-sweet smile, her tangible craving for love and acceptance—it is hard to see what all the fuss was about."[2] Thus, with one gesture, Baker is both fully explicated (a phenomenon that is attributable only to the standing history of eroticizing Black women for white male gaze) and dismissed.

With the centennial of her birth in 2006, there was a resurgence of interest in Baker, including a touring museum exhibit and an academic conference at Columbia University and Barnard College in New York City in the same year and a new US postal stamp in 2008. But views of Baker remain tethered to the vexed poles of vilification and veneration. At the Columbia/Barnard conference, for instance, there was almost unanimous agreement, even if with different intonations, that Baker epitomizes the European history of ethnographic representations. And the issue of Baker's agency invariably becomes mythologized in order to rescue her from the denigrating history that she is seen to unavoidably represent. Similarly, the induction of Baker into the Panthéon two decades later in 2021 focused on her work as a member of the French Resistance, even as the press and social-media responses bifurcated, as they always do, between notes of adulation and disdain. While this history provides an ongoing background for seeing Baker's career, this book traces an alternative, though equally fervent and enduring, context for understanding Baker's iconography and impact.

The phenomenon of Baker is also a phenomenon of modernism and the entwined crises of race, style, and subjecthood. Indeed, how would our understanding of the political expectations surrounding the Black female body be altered were we to consider Baker as a dynamic fulcrum through which the very idea of a "modernist style" is wrought? This study does not claim Baker's modernity as a means of refuting the charges of atavism so frequently leveled at her image. Rather, it takes as a given that modernism and primitivism are intertwined, at times even identical, phenomena.[3] To take this imbrication seriously means that we must expand the contexts and terms through which we approach a figure like Baker.

From its inception, the Baker myth has always generated more visual and categorical conundrum than accepted accounts can accommodate. On the night of October 2, 1925, at the Théâtre des Champs-Élysées, a woman entered the stage on all fours, bottom up, head down, wearing a tattered shirt and cut-off pants, a strange doll among bales of cotton and bandannaed "bucks" and "Black mammies." With her hair slicked back in a shining armor and her mouth painted in minstrel style, this figure started to dance—and danced like nothing anyone had seen before. With eyes crossed, buttocks quivering, legs going every which way, that slim pulsating body onstage appeared part child, part simian, part puppet on neurotic strings; then she retreated. But then she reemerged, this time clad in nothing but copper skin, bright pink feathers around her thighs, ankles, and neck, doing a full split while hanging upside down on the well-oiled shoulders of a Black giant: one moment, dead weight; the next, pure kinetic eruption.

That woman was, of course, Baker. And the show was taking place offstage as well. Records tell us that the audience both sat back and stood, screamed and clapped, shouted at the performer in adoration and disgust; some rushed the stage, while others quit the theater. The next morning, the Parisian papers puzzled over what exactly was seen: "Was she horrible, delicious? Black, white? . . . Woman, other? . . . Dancer, fugitive?"[4] And the mystery did not abate. A year later, *Vanity Fair* continued the fascinating puzzle with a meditation by E. E. Cummings, who revived the performer through a series of rhetorical negations: "a creature neither infrahuman nor superhuman but somehow both: a mysterious unkillable Something, equally nonprimitive and uncivilized, or beyond time in the sense that emotion is beyond arithmetic."[5]

We might take this reception to testify to secret pleasures and their disavowals or chalk it up to the unconscious ambivalence of colonial desire. While these explanations account for the ardor and the contradictions, they cannot quite address the particular terms of this incoherence or why this kind of bewilderment is taking place at this particular time. After almost three centuries of European incursion into the "Dark Continent," more than six decades since the

Emancipation Proclamation in the US, and a quarter of a century into the birth of artistic and literary modernism, which had made much of its attractions for so-called African imports, what we find at this theatrical enactment of two of the most rehearsed sites of European conquest—the plantation and the jungle—is a moment of profound consternation.[6] More intriguingly, it seems worth asking why this consternation, even if disingenuous or exaggerated, should narrate itself specifically as a categorical confusion—that is, over categories of race, gender, and the human that the legacy of imperial history ought to have secured, or at least lent the fantasy of certitude. Thus, at the moment *La Baker* was invented onstage, we see not the affirmation or the denial of modernist primitivism but the failure of its terms to inscribe its own passions.

And, indeed, why Baker? History tells us that chorus girls of every make and model had been strutting up and down the stages of Montmartre for more than a decade by the time she hit the scene in 1925, African American musicians had been arriving in droves since the war, and the Théâtre des Champs-Élysées, unlike its more conservative competitor the Paris Opera, had been catering to the taste for the exotic for years.[7] Still, nothing struck Paris like Baker. The avant-garde's appetite for Baker is the stuff of which legends are made: Jean Cocteau and Miguel Covarrubias designed stage sets and costumes for her, Fernand Léger introduced her to the elite coterie of the Surrealists, Le Corbusier wrote a ballet for her, Henri Matisse made a life-size cutout of her that he hung in his bedroom, Alexander Calder made a wire sculpture of her, Alice B. Toklas invented a pudding recipe named after her, just to cite a few. Beyond designating Baker as the muse, few have been able to articulate what it is about Baker that made her *the* object of such intense and extensive modernist investment.[8] Nor has anyone considered the active interplay (both material and theoretical) between modernist aesthetic practices and the manifest terms of Baker iconography.

So did those audiences see something different—or were they seeing differently? What interests me about revisiting the intimacy between modernism and primitivism is what it can tell us not about how we see racial difference but about how racial difference teaches us *to see.* This line of inquiry is especially important at a time when techniques of seeing are so rapidly changing, for not only do new visual technologies affect how we see racial difference, but, as I will suggest, racial difference itself influences how these technologies are conceived, practiced, and perceived. When we move Baker outside of the well-rehearsed framework of primitivism and juxtapose her celebrated naked skin (as theater and as fabrication) next to other surfaces and other techniques of display in the first quarter of the twentieth century, what we find is a radically different account of what constitutes the Baker phenomenon. What follows, then, is a story of the modern skin and its distractions.

Through the work of Frantz Fanon (especially *Black Skin, White Masks* [1952]), we have come to understand race as an "epidermal schema," as something ineluctably tied to the modality of the visible. Hence, critics like Mary Ann Doane would describe racial difference's "constant visibility" as "inescapable" and as "a disabling overvisibility," and Homi Bhabha would call the indisputable nature of this epidermal scheme colonialism's "open secret," reminding us that "skin, as the key signifier of cultural and racial difference in the stereotype, is the most visible of fetishes."[9] But *is* skin—and its visibility—so available? When we turn to an overexposed and overdetermined figure like Baker, are we in fact seeing what we think we are seeing? What might be some other "schemas" through which skin acquires its legibility? By situating Baker in relation to various modes of modernist display—the stage, photography, film, and architecture—we will trace alternative stories about racialized skin, narratives that compel a reconceptualization of the notions of racialized corporeality, as well as of idealized, modernist facades. It is on the surface of this most organic, sensual, and corporeal of icons that we will find the most unexpected and intense residue of modern synthetics and the imagination that accompanied them.

From the very beginning, Baker's "own skin" offers a highly peculiar business. Although her nakedness has been understood to be a key to her theatrical success and the material evidence of her racial embodiment, it is in fact a remarkably layered construct. In popular cultural memory, her skin is often discursively associated with, at times even rhetorically replaced by, other corporeal habits: banana skins, feathers, drapery. In her films, during the very moments of literal and symbolic exposure, she is also often curiously and immediately covered over by everything from dirt to coal to flour. Arguably one of the most visually remembered entertainers of the twentieth century, Baker frequently appeared in photographs, posters, lithographs, caricatures, and postcards partially or wholly nude, but her nakedness never stands alone and instead frequently exercises an eccentric communion with other epidermises, both natural and inorganic. In short, with Baker, *being unveiled often also means being covered over.*

I want to turn our attention not to what Baker's visibility hides but to how it is that we have failed to see certain things on its surface. In order to broach Baker's skin as a discursive construct and a corporeal agent, we have to first grasp the sediment of signification that "human skin" had accrued by the dawn of the twentieth century. The very substance and contours of the human body were undergoing renovations, a process precipitated by the Industrial Revolution and intensified by the age of mechanical reproduction. Medical advancement, visual technological innovations such as film and photography, and industrial-philosophical discourses such as Taylorism, among other developments, converge to forge a fantasy about a modern, renewed, and disciplined body. At the same time, through discourses such as psychoanalysis, the boundary of the human body is simultaneously multiplied and restricted; the mind/body split gets both literalized and distorted. (Readers of Sigmund Freud will know that his revolutionary discovery of "psychical reality" and the importance of fantasy life itself entail a vexed history of struggle with the tenacious pull of biologism and "fact.")[10] It may not be too much of an overstatement to say that the material and metaphysical boundary of the human body—and, by implication, what constitutes the human—forms one of the central philosophical concerns of the twentieth century.

Perhaps this is why modernism is so obsessed with "skin," its perfection and reproduction in a wide range of discursive and practical spheres and in a startling array of materials. In one of the most whimsical but striking images of modernism, Elie Nadelman's sculpture *Man in the Open Air* (c. 1915, bronze; figure 1.2), we find precisely this dream of perfection.

Our gentleman in the open air is luckily impervious to all atmospheres. He is hermetically sealed in a flawless skin that pours down from his bowler hat through his lithe figure down to his toes, sinking comfortably into the metallic ground: body, vestment,

Fig. 1.2
Is, with that skin, that hair, and those things that pass for lips. Is, with his
way of . . . acting so completely different, from a totally different world.
—*Thomas Glave*

environment as one. Even the tree branch going through his fingers
is not enough to pierce his insouciance but is assimilated instead as an
elegant extension of the body. This sculpture offers a comment about
masculinity, dandyism perhaps, in the fray of modernity. But it also

signals the modernist immersion in the primacy of surface as the perfect corollary to and replacement of human skin. (Did the skin absorb the bronze, or did the alloy absorb the skin?)

The philosophic preoccupation with surface serves as a cornerstone for a host of modernist innovations in a variety of disciplines and forms: in literature, think of Virginia Woolf's description of life as "a semi-transparent envelope" and Oscar Wilde's claim that "only superficial people pay no attention to appearances"; in art, the trajectory from Paul Cézanne's planar surfaces to cubism to Andy Warhol's quip, "If you want to know all about Andy Warhol, just look at the surface"; in architecture, the move from the modernist celebration of blank walls to the "surface talk" that still dominates architectural debates today; in medicine, the new focus on epidermal functions and its semiotics; in science, the accelerated development of scopic technology and the birth of what Hugh Kenner calls "transparent technology."[11] Even in psychoanalysis, there is Freud's reputed methodological shift from what might be called "excavating archaeology" to "surface analysis" or, in the context of conceptualizing the nature of the ego and its ontology, his evocative description of the ego as a "projection of the surface" and, later, Jean Laplanche's depiction of the ego as a "sack of skin."[12] There is, of course, also Didier Anzieu's provocative The Skin Ego (Moi-peau). The trope of skin/surface thus occupies a central place in the making of modern aesthetic and philosophic theory.

To this day, from aerodynamic tears to the glass wall, modern design and aesthetic philosophy remain absorbed in the idea of "pure surface." Contemporary designers continually manipulate the relationship between the inside and the outside of objects, garments, and buildings, creating skins that both reveal and conceal, skins that have depth, complexity, and their own behaviors and identities.[13] Of course, it can be said that all these moves to the surface are not really moves to the surface and in the end reconfirm the surface-depth binary (by, for instance, reproducing the surface as essence). Yet I want to suggest that for a brief period in the early twentieth century, before cultural values collapsed back once again into a (shallow) surface and (authentic) interior divide, there was this tensile and delicate moment when these flirtations with the surface led to profound engagements with and reimagings of the relationship between interiority and exteriority, between essence and covering.

So what *can* the surface be or do if it is not just a cover? This question impacts not only modernist, formalist experimentations but also how the modern history of racialized skin gets seen, read, and written. For we cannot address the history of modern surfaces without also asking after the *other* history of skin, the violent, dysphoric one—the one about racialized nakedness inherited from the Enlightenment so necessary to Western constructions of humanity and the one that speaks of the objectification, commodification, and fetishization of racialized skin, especially Black female skin.[14] While the gendered aspects of modernism's skin preoccupation have been addressed by scholars (Naomi Schor, Mark Wigley), what has been less studied or observed is the element of race in this aesthetic history.[15] In architectural theory, for example, the topic of race rarely arises, yet the skin trope underlying modern architectural conceptions of (white or pure) surface demands a critical engagement with ideas of racial difference. Indeed, as we will see, the question of modern surface itself bears a deeply intimate relationship to the visualization of racialized skin in the twentieth century. The European modernist, aesthetic history of "surface" (that which covers and houses bodies) and the philosophic discourse about "interiority" (that which has been privileged as recessed and essential) provide the very terms on which modern racial legibility in the West, what Fanon calls the "epidermalization of inferiority" is limned.[16]

The relationship between the dress of civilization and the primitive "fact of blackness" (Fanon), moreover, may signal something other than antagonism or disavowal. When aesthetic history meets the history of human bodies made inhuman, what we will confront may be not an account of how modern surface represses or makes a spectacle of racialized skin but, instead, an intricate and inchoative narrative about how the inorganic dreams itself out of the organic and how the organic fabricates its essence through the body of the inanimate. This reciprocal narrative in turn will radically implode the distinction of surface versus essence so central to both racist and progressive narratives about the jeopardized Black body. That is, the perennial opposition between what is open and naked versus what is veiled and hidden has been as important to the racist imagination as it is to the critical intervention designed to decode it. For the racist, nakedness signals rawness, animality, dumb flesh, and is repeatedly invoked, socially and legally, as the sign of the inhuman and the other. For the critical race theorist, that nakedness is deconstructed as an entirely socialized and juridicized concept yet nonetheless reproduced as that which irreducibly indexes skin's visual legibility: "Look, a Negro!"[17] But what happens when we contest the terms of that visibility?

This is where we find Baker, gleaming at the threshold where human skin morphs into modern surface. By actively engaging with the synthetic and covered status of skin, Baker's body as text and performance requires that we reread how we read race. Her reputedly primitive nakedness must be understood within a larger philosophic and aesthetic debate about, and desire for, the "pure surface" that crystallized in the early twentieth century. And that pure surface in turn looks to Black skin, not for disavowal but for articulation. What I am calling the dream of a second skin—of remaking one's self in the skin of the other—is a *mutual* fantasy, one shared both by modernists seeking to be outside of their own skins and by racialized subjects looking to escape the burdens of epidermal inscription. To follow this reciprocal narrative between Black skin and pure surface is to rewrite the story of skin in critical race discourse. Reading modern aesthetic style and Black skin as interrelated and mutually referential holds profound consequences for understanding race as a visual, corporeal phenomenon. By decoupling skin from flesh, the notion of a second skin revises the basic assumptions of a racial discourse that aligns skin with the corporeal and the intractable. The racist interpellation "Look, a Negro!" is thrown into crisis when we attend to the contours of what is seen and when we challenge the most readily available terms of describing the body fixed by that injunction.

What is this thing called race? It is both more and less than biology or ideology. It wields its claim most forcefully and destructively in the realm of the visible, yet it designates and relies on the unseen. Baker, precisely as an apparent racial symbol, counterintuitively and significantly reveals the ellipses and the suspensions preconditioning the stability of that sign. From the inception of early ethnic studies to contemporary critical race theory, so much has been written about skin color in African American literature that other aspects of skin have been neglected. This study revisits the visceral possibilities of raced skin, not in order to recuperate notions of corporeal authenticity but to attend to the curious interface between that skin and inorganic surfaces emerging out of the first quarter of the twentieth century. It tries to understand raced skin as itself a *modern material fascination*, one that speaks not just to a history of objectification but paradoxically also to an emerging concept of matter as mutability, thereby redefining raced skin as "dumb flesh."

For me, the challenge of writing the story of Baker rests in learning how to delineate a material history of race that forgoes the facticity of race. This study is thus not a biography of Baker, nor is it a historiography of her performances. Instead, it offers a series of associative and cumulative meditations about the intimacy between the philosophical origins of the "denuded modern surface" and the theatricalization of "naked skin" at the dawn of the twentieth century, with Baker as a pivotal figure. In these essays, Baker appears, disappears, and reappears to allow into view the enigmas of visual experience that are rarely extended to racialized bodies which remain tied to ideas of visual certitude and readability. We will allow ourselves the gift of itinerancy as we travel through unlikely regions—real stages and imagined houses, banana plantations and ocean liners, metallic bodies and radiant cities—in an effort to track the protean yet ardently persistent conversation between modern surface and Black skin.

The early modernists were in many ways more frank than we are about the seductions and efficacies of otherness in the acts of self-making. Speaking of Baker and the negrophilia sweeping Europe, the poet and novelist Ivan Goll observed in 1926: "But is the Negro in need of us, or are we not sooner in need of her?" There can hardly be a more clear articulation or a more succinct self-diagnosis of European primitivism's need for and projection about the racial other. When it comes to a phenomenon like modernist primitivism, what continues to invite our reading is therefore not colonial ideology's repressed content but its *expressiveness*. What continues to hold our gazes and captivate our minds are those disquieting moments of contamination when reification and recognition fuse, when conditions of subjecthood and objecthood merge, when the fetishist savors his or her own vertiginous intimacy with the dreamed object, and vice versa.

2

In the Museum

Famous for his stylistic incorporation of African artifact and idiom, Pablo Picasso is equally well known for his notorious denial of that influence ("L'art négre? Connais pas!").[1] But in 1937, in an interview with André Malraux, Picasso finally talked about his visit thirty years before in 1907 to the Musée d'Ethnographie du Trocadéro. He described what initially sounds to us today like classic colonial ambivalence:

> When I went to the old Trocadéro, it was disgusting.... But... I stayed. I stayed.... All alone in that awful museum, with masks, dolls made by the redskins, dusty manikins. *Les Desmoiselles d'Avignon* must have come to me that very day.[2]

As is often noted, this famous scene exemplifies how notions of primitive culture, distilled and synecdochized through colonized objects, converge into ideas of violence and femininity.[3] We have no reason to understand Picasso's aversion as anything but colonial desire and its disavowal *until* another ten years later, when in 1947 he returns yet again to this primal scene:

> When I went for the first time . . . to the Trocadéro museum, the smell of dampness and rot there stuck in my throat. It depressed me so much . . . but I stayed . . . I stayed . . . men had made those masks and other objects . . . as a kind of mediation between themselves and the unknown hostile forces that surround them. . . . At that moment I realized what painting was all about . . . a way of seizing the power by giving form to our terrors as well as our desires.[4]

Suddenly, melancholia rather than disgust suffuses the scene.

There are several levels and kinds of identification at work here. There is, of course, the projective and appropriative identification

Second Skin. Second edition. Anne Anlin Cheng, Oxford University Press. © Oxford University Press 2023. DOI: 10.1093/oso/9780197748381.003.0002

assumed by the imperial Western subject: "Oh, I know what those primitive objects are all about..." But the intensity of Picasso's affective response suggests something else as well. Can the "unknown hostile forces" to which Picasso alludes refer to the forces of men as well as of nature? It is difficult not to notice the haunting parallel between "the unknown hostile forces" and the European conquerors who cut those objects off from their contexts in the first place and who relocated those objects to the very museum in which Picasso now stands. Where and what is Picasso's place in this scene? Is it, after all, the objects or the museum (as a mausoleum of Western imperialism) that is dank and rotting? Suddenly, there is a potential identification being drawn between Picasso himself and the "unknown hostile forces" that surrounded and now viewed those objects—which is to say, he has also identified with the objects. What nauseates Picasso may not be disavowal but its failure. In other words, it may be identification, rather than disidentification, that grips Picasso by the throat.

This mythic birth of modern art thus also suggests a moment in which modernism encounters, and is sickened by, its own imperial origins. What Picasso "smells" in the musty ethnography museum may be nothing less than the residue of imperial violence. If art history has told us that modernism meant that objects dismissed by nineteenth-century Europeans as "curios" or "fetishes" had suddenly become crucial to the twentieth-century artists searching for new form (William Rubin, Marianna Torgovnick), here Picasso's account opens up the space for remembering the cultural, mercantile, and political violence that enables the processes through which these stranded objects were initially infused with magic and then transformed into corpses. What struck Picasso with such psychical force may be less the objects than the histories that made those objects "objects."

This is not to say that invidious appropriation was not a major mode of modernist primitivism, but it is to note that acts of appropriation also open up sites of contamination that point to other kinds of relationality, ones that may not always be easily categorized. Alongside taking in the objects, Picasso was also taken by the objects. In addition to exercising spectatorship, he was also shattered by it. What Picasso took from the museum may not be the fetish objects per se but their logic, a logic that traces the fundamentally melancholic relationship between subjects and objects, a relationship that imperial desire amplifies to its extreme and that modernism (from surrealism to objectivism) cannot cure. These decontextualized fragments collected in the Trocadéro register the ways in which objects reference culture and the subjects that animate them and yet, at the same time, remain inert to those affective investments. In short, objects promise life—what Soaphead Church in Toni Morrison's *The Bluest Eye* calls "the residue of human spirits"[5]—but they also embody/embalm the signs of that life's passing, or its failure to stick.

It is the violation of Picasso's own psychical boundary—that rupture in his throat—that transports him from a position of mastery into one of crisis. The euphoria of remastery in the face of this rupture ("a way of seizing . . . power") cannot quite dispel the haunting fact that these objects' presence in the museum testifies to their failures as talismans. Relics are, after all, preeminently that paradox: *dead objects*, the material things left over after the symbolic meanings imbued in them have disappeared. In being the physical residue of meaning, the memory of that signification, these objects are like human corpses whose materiality exceeds human life itself, to people's horror and celebration. The force of this museum encounter therefore suggests not only that objects hold an insufficient or uncanny relationship to the subjective investments repeatedly attributed to them but also the shattering possibility that the spectacle of objecthood might remind us of *the husks that we are*: the vertiginous reminder that so much of our own cherished subjectivity is borrowed magic, that our subjecthood bears unbearable proximity to objecthood.

And now we arrive at yet another line of identification in this scene: the correlation between the act of painting and the shells of those remains. If Picasso enjoyed a sudden euphoria in consequence of his melancholic identification with the dead objects, it is not the elation of compensatory mastery (how I can stop feeling like those objects) but that of identification (how I can *be* like those objects). Indeed, we might say that the birth of Picasso's reputed signature style gestures to a fundamental—even an *orthopedic*—likeness between canvas/modern surface and the husks of non-Western bodies: the "masks," "redskin dolls," and "manikins." The nature of agency derived from this surface identification is specific and peculiar: the act of painting "seizes power" *not* by dispelling threats but by "giving form" to terror and desire. In other words, painting does not fend off violent invasion, nor does it revive that which has been killed. Instead, it, like relics, congeals ("giving form to") the memory of violence. The canvas becomes artifact, testifying to desire and its trauma. Action emerges not in the shape of mastery but in the shadow of enclosure. Cubic preoccupation with surface originates at this moment when Picasso sees painting as a means of embalmment, one whose function serves *not* to reify or revive but to *record loss in the wake of reification*. Thus, what has traditionally been taken as an instance of colonial projection and disgust turns out to be a passionate confrontation with colonial fantasy's violent preconditions.

Although art historians have long debated the formal characteristics of how tribal objects get reincorporated into modern art, what we are witnessing here are the profound ways in which the residual skins of dead, racialized objects initiate not only a reorganization of the modern artist's visual field but also his psychical borders.[6] The effect of the "primitive" object on the modern subject is not only one of stylistic influence but also one of onto-visual realignment. In this museum encounter, the cover of the stranded object reorganized how the subject saw. If what Picasso learned at the ethnography museum was a way of seeing—"what painting was all about"—then it was also a vision that understood seeing not as a mastery of surface but as its agent. We do not master by seeing; we are ourselves altered when we look.

3

Skins, Tattoos, and the Lure
of the Surface

Pablo Picasso was not the only modernist who discovered his art
through the skin of the other. In one of the founding moments of
modern architectural theory, we find the skin of the other playing an
equally unexpected and critical role. In his 1898 essay "The Principle
of Cladding," Adolf Loos (1870–1933), one of the founding fathers of
modern architecture and a Viennese contemporary of Sigmund Freud,
attributes the origin of architecture not to structure or solid material, as might be expected, but to mobile surfaces: fabric, even skin.
Elaborating on his dictum *Im Anfang war die Bekleidung* ("In the beginning was clothing"), he writes:

> In the beginning was cladding [*Bekleidung*]. . . . The covering is the
> oldest architectural detail. Originally it was made out of animal skins
> or textile products. This meaning of the word [*Decke*] is still known
> today in the German languages. Then the covering had to be put up
> somewhere if it were to afford enough shelter. . . . Thus the walls were
> added. . . .[But] cladding is even older than structure.[1]

For Loos, *Bekleidung*/"cladding" connotes the covering of both
bodies and buildings by additional layers. In his view, architecture
bears more kinship to fabric than to masonry. Walls are really of sec-
ondary concern and come into being only as an afterthought and a
structural necessity. We might say that for Loos, structure stands as the
material embodiment of ghostlier and keener demarcations.

Loos's emphasis on architecture's "skin" origin, however, proves to
be something of a theoretical conundrum for him. Although he takes
his ideas about the primacy of cladding (and even the term *Bekleidung*)
from the German historian and architect Gottfried Semper, who made

Second Skin. Second edition. Anne Anlin Cheng, Oxford University Press. © Oxford University Press 2023.
DOI: 10.1093/oso/9780197748381.003.0003

the initial connection between skin and textile in architectural theory (Semper believed that textile was the primary stimulus for all figuration in both architecture and art and considered tattoos and human bodily adornment to be the first arts), Loos departs radically from his teacher when he develops an allergy to primitive arts, especially the tattoo.[2] In his other well-known essay, pithily titled "Ornament and Crime" (1908), Loos summarily dismisses ornamentation in architectural practice, laying the philosophical basis for the ideal of the denuded modern surface. Labeling the nineteenth-century secessionist penchant for architectural covering as useless, pathological, degenerate, and criminal, Loos compares such preferences to "the [childish and amoral] tattoos of the Papuan."[3] According to Loos, as modern men mature and evolve, they must also learn to relinquish the regressive pleasures of ornamentation. The march of progress is thus equated with the suppression and erasure of erotic material excess, deemed to be the exclusive and natural domains of sexual and savage primitives, such as (in Loos's words) "negroes, Arabs, rural peasants," and, of course, "women and children."[4]

"Ornament and Crime" stands as a foundational text in the development of modern architectural theory, providing the basis for a long trajectory of modernist preoccupation with the idea of clean surfaces, culminating in Le Corbusier's resolute call for the ubiquity of a coat of opaque whitewash: his "Law of Ripolin."[5] For these innovators of modern architecture, the ideal of architectural purity—defined as specifically the liberation from "primitive" and "feminine" inclinations—is inextricably bound to the twin ideals of culture and civilization. This version of architectural anthropology bears close resemblance to Freud's notion of human development and to its conflation of ontogeny and phylogeny.[6] For Freud, Loos, and, half a generation later, Le Corbusier, "man" becomes civilized—and his surroundings modernized—by renouncing primitive proclivities. The discourse of the "pure" modern surface thus produces a nexus of metonymic meanings—purity, cleanliness, simplicity, anonymity, masculinity, civilization, technology, intellectual abstractism—that are set off against notions of excessive adornment, inarticulate sensuality, femininity, backwardness. This dream of an undistracted surface will impact not only the development of modern architectural theory but also stylistic revolutions in the diverse fields of art, literature, fashion, commercial design, and technology. To this day, we uphold some of the most basic tenets of this ideal in our celebration of the "tasteful" (in our language, clothing, and everyday objects) as the sleek, the understated, and the unadorned.

This undistracted surface, however, is not without its distractions, just as this renunciation of style is, of course, also itself a style and one that is particularly *thick*. Even as Loos denigrates "primitive" tastes, he could never fully relinquish his attachment to what he sees as architecture's originary function. Throughout his career, he insists that architecture embody and memorialize its crucial role as primal cover: what José Quetglas i Riusech calls Loos's "architecture of the womb."[7] It will therefore not surprise the reader that the corpus of Loos's architectural projects exhibits a kind of "splitting." While his buildings are known for their sparse and anonymous facades, the interiors often reveal a shamelessly extravagant penchant for the sensual delights of textile coverings, hangings, and other extraneous details. There are, for example, the completely fur- and fabric-lined walls, floor, and furniture of the bedroom he designed for his second wife, Lina, and himself in Vienna, a uterine dream of inverted animal skin.

Critics have mapped this apparent paradox in Loos onto the split between (masculinized and impassive) exteriors and (feminized and sensuous) interiors. Alan Colquhoun, for instance, writes in his foundational introduction, *Modern Architecture*, that

> Externally, Loos's villas were cubes without ornamentation. . . . Loos was making a conscious analogy with modern urban man, whose standardized dress conceals his personality and protects him from the stress of the modern metropolis. But, in Loos's houses, once he has penetrated the wall, this "man of nerves" is enmeshed in a "feminine" and sensuous complexity, full of those residues of cultural memory and association that have been banished from the building's exterior.[8]

This reading would be consistent with the ideas of sociologist Georg Simmel, whom Loos also read and who argued that the modern metropolis and its anonymous architecture are designed to protect

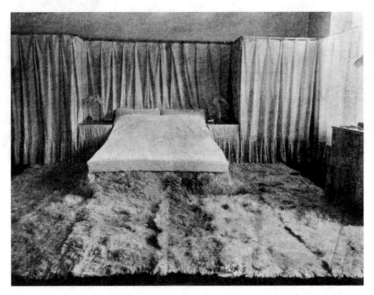

Fig. 3.1
[T]he metropolitan type of man . . . develops an organ protecting him
against the threatening currents and discrepancies of his external
environment.
—*Georg Simmel*

men.[9] Yet if we look at "Lina's Bedroom" (figure 3.1), the posited
distinction between interiority and exteriority—as well as between
femininity and masculinity—may not be as clean as critics, or Loos,
would prefer.

Loos explicitly named this room "Lina's Bedroom," as if to underscore his separation from this feminized space; yet his own unspoken presence and, presumably, enjoyment in that room, of course,
gestures to a deeper intimacy with that uterine space. Thus, on the one
hand, this room exemplifies the womblike nature of Loos's architecture; as Quetglas once prescribed: "All the architecture of Loos can
be explained as the envelope of the body."[10] On the other hand, this
"womb" or "envelope" is inverted and even potentially ruptured. Is
this room or womb designed to *wrap around* or *stand in for* the body?
And what do we do with those furs anyway? Are they skin or hide?
Cladding or decoration? Lush or raw?

And here we come to the central conundrum in Loos's theoretical work. When it comes down to it, what distinguishes cladding from ornamentation? What is essence, and what is auxiliary? The divide between covering and ornamentation, between intellectual form and degenerate eroticism, turns out to be neither simple nor stable for this sensual aesthete.[11] And the problem rests precisely on the idea of "skin" and its inherently complicated relation to essence versus surface. Skin is, after all, by nature a medium of transition and doubleness: it is at once surface and yet integrally attached to what it covers. It also serves as a vibrant interface between the hidden and the visually available. Yet the status of skin in this room highlights all the instabilities inherent in this membrane, underscoring its potential for disruptions rather than its capacity for transition. Those furs remind us not only of skin's warmth and luxury but also of its violence. That is, they also suggest the ominous aspects of the room-as-womb: not safe encasement (the skin against skin of the mother-child dyad) but the imminent threat of tearing, flaying, and displacement. The comforting return to maternal skin is achieved at the price of, or exists simultaneously with, the reminders of flayed and displaced skin.

Moreover, these skins and furs, traditionally objects of feminized ornamentation (which in turn connotes the animality of femininity), also impact the boundaries of masculinity. We might want to ask, what do these furs do to or for the man in that room? More than simply providing shelter (in the way that Simmel talks about the need to shelter man from the onslaught of modern life), Loos seems intent on producing a second skin for man, one that simultaneously and paradoxically covers and denudes him. Beatriz Colomina, who has produced some of the most intriguing readings of Loos's work, has astutely observed that Loos's interiors are more theatrical than comforting, that they enact a tension between voyeurism and self-exposure.[12] Let us locate that tension within the very notion of a Loosian surface. With "Lina's Room," that which is decorative appears to be also structural and structuring; and the feminized and the feral are not so much repressed as spectacularly invoked. So if we see the Loosian villa as an analogy for man himself, then this house is something of a double cross-dresser: a vulnerable man wearing his animalized femininity inside out, which is in turn reencased by the mask of impassive masculinity. Colquhoun's phrase "man of nerves" now takes on a teasing doubleness: nerves of steel or tender, exposed nerves? The problem, as we begin to suspect, is that the facade may not have banished what Colquhoun called those "feminine and sensuous residues" so much as reproduced them, nor has interiority been fully restrained from enacting surface activity.

Loos's celebrated design innovation, known as the *Raumplan*, also reveals this double inclination to skin (in both senses of enveloping and stripping) the body. The *Raumplan* embodies a complex system of internal organization that culminates in Loos's famous split-level house designs. According to Loos, the architect's starting point should not be structural dividers but volume and mass: "My architecture is not conceived in plans, but in spaces (cubes). I do not design floor plans, facades, sections. I design spaces."[13] Loos's interest in *voluminous surface* signals a preoccupation with not only economy and functionality, as is often noted, but also the flow of space (characterized by split-level floors and interpenetrating spaces) and its ability to envelope the inhabitant and shape his or her experience within space. That is, the combination of surface and volume affords the human subject the experience of a container or an envelope—this is why Loos's interiors are so often described as womblike. We might say that architectural volume's relationship to the human subject functions for Loos in much the same way as what psychoanalyst Didier Anzieu called the "Skin Ego." Building on Freud's 1923 essay on "The Ego and the Id," where Freud famously and enigmatically asserts that the ego "is itself the projection of a surface," Anzieu highlights the role played by skin and argues that the ego is primarily structured as a "Skin Ego." For Anzieu, "the ego is the projection on the psyche of the surface of the body," and the skin ego is "a mental image of which the ego of the child makes use . . . as an ego containing psychical contents."[14]

Note the architectural/spatial metaphors underlying Anzieu's work. Both Loos and Anzieu were preoccupied by the notion of an envelope for the body, a container that effects an active negotiation linking space to body to ego. For the architect and analyst alike, the *container* determines—or even engenders—the content. For Anzieu, the infant acquires the perception of a bodily surface through contact with the skin of the mother or caretaker.[15] The ego thus does not consist of pre-existing psychical content but comes into being only via the making of a psychical container, a process that is built on the infant's "experience of the surface of the body."[16] In short, the house of the ego determines its content. For Loos, architectural design proceeds from a similar logic: volume produces surface that in turn enables the potentiality of human *presence* and *occupation*.

Yet how safe is the human ego in the envelope of the *Raumplan*? Where a classical plan endorses an a priori system of expectations about how one moves through a house, the *Raumplan* in contrast enacts what Colquhoun describes as a "spatial-temporal labyrinth."[17] To occupy this spatial-temporal labyrinth surely implies degrees of peril as well as liberty. We might consider, for instance, how those continuous yet split levels at once elongate and delay bodily movement, and on the level of the gaze, how they potentially draw the visitor's vision even as they impede a comprehension of the structure as a whole. Visual mastery would be at once solicited and denied. All this makes the Loosian interior a curious study in tension. Colquhoun has noted that the so-called open plan is composed of "hermetic cubes" that are "difficult to penetrate" and that the spatial continuity in the *Raumplan* is often achieved by "piercing" the walls with wide openings and framed views.[18] Frequently what connect the rooms are visual elements of framing, what Colquhoun compares to "a proscenium."[19] This peculiar tension between openness and impenetrability, between privacy and staging, between body and its framing has led Colomina to wittily observe that in a Loos interior someone always seems to be about to make an entrance.[20] This theatricality, however, has a particularly suspended component about it: the body is always wrapped and protected yet also on the verge of presentation and exposure. We are in essence talking not quite of a "womb" or a theater but of a hybrid in between: a *pregnant volume*, one that produces not only containment but also latency and immanence and one that turns presence into promise and a haunting.

The curious envelope of the Loosian structure will provide the basis for a set of related problems about "modern skin" that we will pursue, but it is worth stepping back and noting that the "primitive skin" constitutes a source both of intense creativity and of acute allergy for Loos's architectural bodies. This kind of ambivalence is, of course, profoundly characteristic of the discursive practice of primitivism—and, for that matter, of that of modernism and of psychoanalysis. Some of the most exciting work done on the legacies of psychoanalysis has demonstrated the entangled relationship of psychoanalysis and European colonial desire.[21] What I want to point out here is that at the imbricated conjunction of colonialism, modernity, and psychoanalysis, we are also seeing a very peculiar vision of the human body and of its exterior containment. Precisely at the culmination of decades of the systematic objectification of the racial "other" and after a century of fascination with classification and difference born out of the thought of Charles Darwin, Arthur de Gobineau, and Francis Galton, imaginations about the European body were paradoxically becoming increasingly mediated and haunted. Similarly, just as the boundary of the bourgeois body was coming into its distinctive outline in scientific and medical discourse, the limits of that borderline became contestable.[22] For Freud, the formation of the ego will become more and more indebted to, and vexed by, a history of digested and undigested bodies. (The Freudian ego, after all, is never a solitary affair.) And for Loos, the very idea of structure itself embodies architecture's internal ambivalence about the enterprise of keeping bodies separate from covers.

When we take a closer look at the theoretical writings of this father of modern architecture, we find the unadorned surface to be not so much repressing as *housing* the very "primitive" ghosts that it denounces. With Loosian *Bekleidung*, we are looking at not a case of repression but an instance of *impersonation*. The undecorated, anonymous facade was meant to provide a protective shield for modern man, but what that covering is made of is a different matter. The affinity between the denuded surface and the raw naked skin renders the Loosian surface an expression of simultaneity rather than denial. To put it differently, Loos rejects the tattooing of the body, but he has replaced that gesture with the building itself, which is seen as a cover grafted onto the body. Is Loos's turn to the blank wall simply an evasion or a denial of primitive inclinations? Not quite—or rather, if it is, it is evasion that memorializes, a disavowal that announces itself.

The problem of the modern surface—that is, the heuristic and critical problem of distinguishing decoration as surplus from what is "proper" to the thing—will hold profound implications for both the theorization of modern buildings and that of modern, raced bodies.

By seeing architecture as an enactment of skin-upon-the-skin, Loos simultaneously replaces and displaces the exterior integument of the "modern man." We are, in other words, in the terrain of fetishism in both the anthropological and psychological registers. The racial fetish, metonymized as animal or Papuan skin in Loos's work, provides the pivot on which modernist aesthetic values turn: essence versus veneer, plainness versus excess, utility versus waste, taste versus vulgarity. Yet, as we have started to see, the pivot—that haunting skin—is itself already contaminated. Modern architecture may in fact be quite naked, though not in the senses of purity or transparency, as is traditionally claimed, but rather in the very material sense of embodying a profound nostalgia for, if not a downright imitation of, the lost, originary, naked skin. (Is this, like Picasso's canvas, another instance of embalmment rather than reification?) Thus, at the birth of modern plastic arts in the age of mechanical reproduction, the invention and sanctification of the newly minted, denuded modern surface itself bears the incrustations of a layered history about the imaginary and material presence of "primitive skin."

4

What Bananas Say

It is out of the embroiled tension between fabricated nakedness and dreamed covering that Josephine Baker emerges as one of the highest-paid entertainers in theatrical history. So why should we approach a burlesque star through the lens of architectural theory? What do buildings have to do with bodies? As we have started to see, quite a lot, actually. First, in being linked and likened to surrogate and "primitive" skin, building surface has become the charged site for raising larger questions about the modern body, its boundaries, and its essence. Second, our initial encounter with Adolf Loos has shown us that "cover" and "lack" are key terms in the theoretical machinery behind the making of the smooth, "naked," modern surface. Modernist rejection of the nineteenth-century fetishization of ornamentation turns out to rely on a fetishization of bareness. From one perspective, this new bareness is but another version of essence; essence has merely been displaced from interiority to exteriority. (Call to mind here those modernist buildings that expose their interior structures.) But it would be misguided to think that the notion of essence has been preserved or reborn without challenge, for it is precisely in that move, that relocation from inside out, that the very structure supporting the distinction between essence/interiority and cover/exteriority begins to turn in on itself. In the fetishizing of surface, an implosion occurs within the structure itself.

As Loos struggled over the meaning of architectural "covers," bodies were also being made, denuded, and unveiled elsewhere, in particular, the theatrical culture of the striptease in the early twentieth century.[1] It may not be a coincidence that the denuded modern surface and the theater of the striptease (both modes of displaying the body) both came into being at the dawn of the twentieth century. If, as I am suggesting, the story of modern architecture is also a story about the dramatic encounter between European whiteness and its racial others,

Second Skin. Second edition. Anne Anlin Cheng, Oxford University Press. © Oxford University Press 2023. DOI: 10.1093/oso/9780197748381.003.0004

then nowhere does that encounter play itself out as spectacularly as on the stages of European dance halls, theaters, and cinema, where the fetishism of the visual constructs its vocabulary with extravagant relish and where the boundary between bodies and things both asserts itself and becomes threatened.

The striptease, as a particularly modern form of mass entertainment, provides a crucial locus for examining how exposed skin—as a synecdoche for race, sex, and other signs of social difference—becomes the preeminent ground of contestation over the meaning of those categories. The origins of stripping as a performance art are much disputed, and various dates and occasions have been given, from ancient Babylonia to twentieth-century America.[2] *The People's Almanac*, for instance, credits the origin of the striptease in France to an act in the 1890s in Paris in which a woman slowly removed her clothes supposedly in search for a flea crawling on her body. At around the same time, venues such as the Moulin Rouge and the Folies Bergère were pioneering seminude dancing and tableaux vivants. For our purpose here, the first note of observation to be made points to the historical and formal affinity that the genre of the striptease bears to nineteenth-century pseudoscientific display. Indeed, we might see that urgently sought-after yet potentially wholly imaginary little flea as the perfect alibi for or symptom of the historical and specular display of the female (especially lower-class) body: standing in as the justification for the masculine, medical, and hygienic gaze even as it functions as the very sign of feminine and primitive contamination. It is no coincidence that the striptease becomes a recognizable theatrical genre at the height of European primitivism, nor is it surprising that the theatrical idiom of venues such as the Moulin Rouge and the Folies Bergère would favor what might be called the "zoological."[3] Racialized and feminized nudity in turn serves as a primary conceit in this visual vocabulary emerging from European primitivism. The simultaneously scientific and prurient display of such nakedness—in letters, early daguerreotypes, and postcards and through the inception and dissemination of journals such as *National Geographic*—has been central to the imperial and colonial projects of European expansion.

It is, however, crucial not only to understand the idea of modern nakedness in the context of that imperial (hence racialized and sexualized) history but also to explore the ways in which the making of that nakedness confounds that very history as unitary or masterful. The transition from ethnography to mass cultural entertainment may not be as easy or "natural" as it initially seems. Yes, they share a theatrical logic. Yes, they both objectify and spectacularize the racialized body. Yet mass entertainment forms such as the burlesque stage—and, soon to follow, the cinema—also produce very different relations between the subject and object of gaze, as well as altering the viewing process.

The burlesque theater, unlike the ethnographic study, has no obligation to the illusions of objectivity or science. Its format explicitly calls for the circulation of desire and draws its audience to performance. (Think about those shouting viewers at the Théâtre des Champs-Élysées.) And the advent of cinema also demanded a different kind of looking. We will explore this in more detail later when we look at Baker's films, but for now my point is a modest one: to grasp the impact of Baker stripping on the stages of the Théâtre des Champs-Élysées and the Folies Bergère and in film, we have to go beyond the colonial history of ethnographic display. As we are about to see, in spite of drawing from that historical vocabulary, Baker may be said to represent a significant rupture in that history because the *modes* of display that made her image famous have changed.

The spectacularization of skin onstage at the turn of the twentieth century, instead of simply fulfilling a trajectory of colonial representation, also reveals how the textures of those representations transform and are transformed by the making of "modern nakedness," be it on buildings or bodies. I concentrate on the early part of Baker's career, the part that made her name and the part that is much harder to assimilate into the latter narrative of her life as celebrated war hero and civil rights activist. For many fans, it is in the latter part of her career when she took up an explicit, liberal agenda that redeems her legacy.[4] But I want to take us back to a period when the question of her politics is much more vexed in order to apply pressure on what constitutes agency versus spectacle at the much more unruly site of expressive racial and sexual fantasy. The '20s and '30s were crucial theatrical moments for Baker because that was when she performed most regularly in the nude or seminude and when she was supposed to be catering most visibly to the European tradition of racialized displays. And indeed, the publicity of her political activities during World War II and in the 1960s acquires its piquancy often precisely because of its supposed contrast with her early and, shall we say, more wicked fame.

Celebrated as icon and decried as fetish, Baker has been viewed as either a groundbreaking performer or a shameful sellout.[5] Instead of resolving these tensions, I am more interested in the challenges to the politics of the visible that her work and legacy pose. The contours of racial difference at the site and sight of the most racialized stage may surprise us. While it may be said that many aspects of Baker's performances—from her lyrics to her choreography to her costumes— draw insistent attention to the very notion of the fetish, both racial and sexual, this observation, instead of saying something about Baker her- self or about her politics, in fact provokes a series of questions about the convergence of style, history, and performance and about how fet- ishism as a mode of partial recognition feeds into the politics of that convergence.

To make inroads into this complex of interpenetrating issues about art, exposure, race, sex, imperialism, and contemporary critique, let us begin by considering what might be called Baker's relentless self- fetishization. Baker was not just a Black female performer; she was a performer who relentlessly enacted fantasies of Black femininity. We might say that fetishism was the theme *and* the mode of her career. In pieces such as "Chocolate Dandies" (figure 4.1), Baker drew from the minstrel tradition.

In another famous performance known as the *danse sauvage* (figure 4.2), Baker burned herself into Parisian cultural memory by appearing onstage barely covered in a pink feather loincloth, doing a full split while hanging upside down from the arms of her giant of a partner, Joe Alex.

There remains much to be said about these images, as we will see later, but for now I want to invoke them as preliminary examples of how Baker actively solicits stereotypical expectations. These iconic images exemplify colonial ambivalence (the idealization of primitive innocence and the denigration of primitive sexuality), and their re- ception today (as evidence of either her naive victimization by or her calculated parody of European racism and sexism) must be seen as

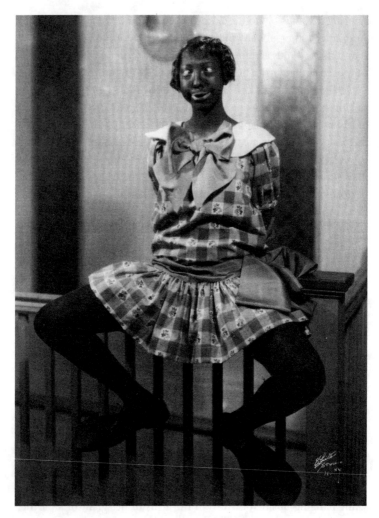

Fig. 4.1

continuing, rather than intervening in, this discourse of ambivalence.[6] The interesting question is not one of Baker's agency (indeed, the question of her self-construction or self-representation is complex by nature, given her professional obligations and the social world in which she succeeded) but how the terms of agency and performance must be nuanced in a context where the question of consent is seriously

Fig. 4.2

compromised. The attribution of subversive intentionality on the part of Baker, as some critics are wont to give, does not get us away from the problem that when it comes to the spectacle of the stereotype, execution and parody look uncomfortably similar. As a handful of critics have started to show us, Baker's style is a hybrid and complicated phenomenon, one that warns us against the shortsightedness of perceiving this performer as solely a representative of European ethnographic display.[7] Subversion, after all, replays rather than sidesteps the fetish. So how do we understand Baker's relationship to racial and gender fetishism?

Nothing says fetish like Baker's infamous banana-skirt dance. At the height of her career, Baker performed at the Folies Bergère,

Fig. 4.3
It is the purest nakedness. And an absolute disguise.
—*Gail Jones*

appearing onstage wearing next to nothing but a little skirt of plush bananas (figure 4.3).[8] It is the outfit with which she would be identified for the rest of her life. Consider, for example, Harryette Mullen's short prose poem:

> In feathers, in bananas, in her own skin, intelligent body attached to a gaze. Stripped down model, posing for a savage art, brought to color to a primitive stage.[9]

Even non–Baker fans would recognize the unnamed apparition in Mullen's words by the telltale bananas. But both the poem as a piece of writing and the figure that it describes may be more peculiar than the terse language suggests. Are we looking at a person or a replica? Is she (or it) being stripped down or dressed up? Whose gaze? And what kind of a body is it anyway that wears feathers and bananas like second skins?

I am not interested in claiming "Baker-turned-ornamentation" as either the sign of her objectification or the evidence of her subversive agency or some simplistic notion of self-invention. Instead, I want to concentrate on the details and textures of those ornamentations and ask questions about what that "style" is itself doing in relation to the supposed "real" body that it covers. The complication of subject and object, and of person and thing, in Mullen's poem raises a set of questions about how we understand the "stage" of primitivist performances, especially when it enters the realm of explicit theatricality. When "scientific object" turns into "performer," agency becomes simultaneously flaunted and constrained.

So what *are* those bananas saying? To begin with, those famous bananas, cited on both sides of the Atlantic to this day (from Mullen's poetry to Suzanne Lori-Parks's theater to Paris Métro ads to Beyoncé's recitation), would seem to be the most obvious symbol there is for a racist and sexist joke. But what exactly is the joke? Are the bananas girding Baker's loins a phallic or a racial allusion? Is the white audience hungry for the bananas or the lack they disguise? (It is not a coincidence that journalistic and critical accounts of those bananas would alternately record them as either flaccid or turgid.)[10] Is it the banana or is it the skirt that is the object of fetishistic investment for the white male audience, and what of the white female audience, of which there were plenty? Is the skimpy skirt a sign of civilization or of its inadequacy? What about her male counterpart, Joe Alex, in all his naked, muscular Blackness?

And if we think about those bananas as also signifying colonial commerce and its rapacious appetite (for it was in the 1920s that banana plantations were being promoted as a supplement to and replacement for the sugar plantations in the French Antilles), then what exactly is being consumed in this dizzyingly layered scene, where the object of enjoyment is a prized but easily bruised "exotic" fruit masking the Black female lack masking the Black dick masking the hunger of the white imperial phallus?[11] Finally, let us not forget that it is entirely possible that Baker herself got (a different) pleasure out of her witty costume. In short, what exactly is the fetish in this scene, and for whom?

All these questions are invoked by the banana skirt, haunting the spectacle being offered. It is precisely these multiple possibilities that highlight the epistemological crisis engendered by the fetishistic system. The move from a psychological conceptualization of sexual fetishism to the vernacular notion of racial fetishism is itself problematic. We recall that the Freudian fetish, which was exclusively a sexual pathology, functions for heterosexual men as a kind of psychical lubricant in the face of castration anxiety by making the supposed horror of female castration bearable, thereby enabling the fulfillment of normative male desire: "[fetishism] endow[s] women with the characteristic which makes them tolerable as sexual objects."[12] But then the question obviously arises: is the heterosexuality ensured by fetishism an ability to enjoy the woman as woman or as man? Either way, so-called normal male heterosexuality begins to look like anything but a given. Thus, the Freudian fetish is a psychical process designed to segregate sexual differences that in fact registers the horrors of the permeability of that difference.

Sexual fetishism, as originally identified by Freud, is thus itself already a highly unstable structure, and when we take this sexual paradigm and map the racial onto it, the instabilities proliferate exponentially. Thus, while, as Homi Bhabha points out, there are both structural and functional justifications for thinking about racial stereotypes as specifically a form of fetishism,[13] this equation nonetheless leaves several unresolved remainders. Indeed, given the peculiar specificities of Freudian sexual fetishism, the transposition of the racial onto the sexual paradigm becomes harder and harder to map with accuracy. What are the terms of disavowal, displacement, and replacement when it comes to the scene of the cross-racial encounter? As we saw with the banana skirt, the dynamic of lack and compensation generates a host of complications when we combine racial anxiety with sexual anxiety. The two forms of anxiety are not merely parallel or additive as they are often thought to be.

My point here is not to be a literalist but to highlight the ways in which what does not fit in the translation between racial and sexual fetishism indexes precisely those aspects of the conjunction between race and sexuality that we have yet to account for in the liberal telling of that intersection. If Baker is seen as offering up a classic spectacle of racialized femininity for the white heterosexual male gaze, then she is also serving up that femininity armed with a ring of embarrassingly fruitful phalluses. (Baker herself, in the course of her career, courted her androgyny as much as she played up her ultrafemininity.) The effects of that fantasmatic "phallus" on the desiring European audience not only invoke the homoerotic undertones of heterosexual desire but also cross over into the colonial register: one would also have to confront the possibility that this now phallic maternal body holds as well an uncomfortable affinity to Black masculinity, the "ape" to which the bananas allude. And if one sees the skirt as a domestication of Baker's jungle ways, then one must also confront the fact that civilized Blackness flaunts a set of (flaccid or taut?) bananas.

Is the object of enjoyment, finally, the Black woman or her fantasmatic Black masculinity? Does enjoyment here denote desire or identification or both?[14] When Baker's supposed lack gets transposed onto her abundant bananas, then what is there to protect the white male audience from her gaping yet protruding Blackness? Instead of conferring stable racial or sexual meaning in the face of uncertainty, these contradictory significations foreground the crisis of meaning in the fetish *and* in the cross-cultural exchange between European whiteness and the "other." Instead of establishing a clear-cut dichotomy between viewer and view, subject and object, master and slave, the mise-en-scène actually enables and encapsulates a complex network of mediated desires and cross-narratives. If we see the Baker-banana-Alex

collaboration as a fantasy tableau, the viewer's entry point into it is significantly multiple. This suggests that the pleasures of racial fetishism
for the fetishist (be that the master or the slave) are *not* that they protect one from racial otherness but that they launch one into an imaginary scenario where one gets to *have* and *be* that otherness.[15]

And given that this is a performance written, staged, and
choreographed by an African American troupe and financially
underwritten by a white New York socialite with expressed intentions
to cater to a French aesthetic of Africanity, with a set design by the
Mexican artist Miguel Covarrubias, we have to wonder whether the
resulting mise-en-scène might reveal not only a mediated white imagination about Blacks but also its inverse. Similarly, we must take into
account the mediating roles of fantasies of the Americas about the
Continent and vice versa. The theater format actually disguises the cir-
cularity of specular exchange that in fact informs those performances.
And it is precisely the intertwined dynamics of identification and
disidentification, of projection and self-location, feeding the fetish
structure that marks the fetishistic exchange as a political one. The
staging of the racial fetish throws into relief rather than appeases the
problematic distinction of segregating Blackness from whiteness,
cover from exposure, masculinity from femininity, civilization from
brutality.

This built-in failure of every successful fetish construction holds
profound implications for how we understand the subject and object
of discrimination. The racial fetish disrupts instead of clarifies the
distinction between master and object, between control and tumult.
Thus, the fetish always embodies a residue of its own renunciation, and
it is only from this remainder (rather than Baker's personal intentions)
that we can construct a political and critical evaluation of this historic
performance. The banana skirt, with its supposedly transparent (racial and erotic) joke, stands as both a reduction and a redundancy in
the allegorical network embedded in the scene. It sutures—flimsily, we
might add—the unwieldy cycle of identification and disidentification
unleashed in the encounter between the supposed subject and the object of primitivism. Baker offers not only a case study or a symbol of

colonial projection but also an embodiment of the very crisis of differentiation founding that imperial desire.

Somewhere between fetish and fact, the twin poles to which women of color seem invariably consigned, are the murky and intriguing places where pleasure, insight, objectification, and subjection come into mutual articulation. The staging of the fetish—be it Picasso's relics or Loos's Papuan skin or Baker's bananas—never secures subjective mastery, as is often thought, but initiates instead a vertiginous renegotiation of subjecthood and objecthood. It is on the stage of contaminated desires that we are most pressed to reconsider the politics of recognition.[16]

5

Housing Baker, Dressing Loos

In 1926, after the theatrical imprint of her banana skirt on European memory, a young Josephine Baker, still flushed from the explosion of her European debut, met a middle-aged architect, Adolf Loos. Based on a rather superficial acquaintance, Loos designed a house for Baker (figure 5.1).[1]

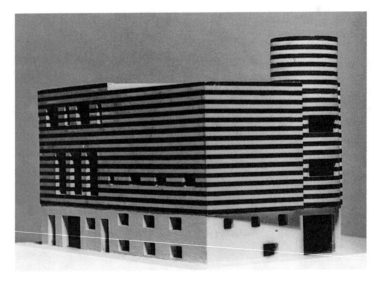

Fig. 5.1

The house was never built, but the design remains notable in architectural history. Let us begin our virtual tour and step inside its imaginary walls.

The inside of this house is as arresting as its exterior. Loos once said that the architect is not an artist but simply a "stonemason who has learned Latin."[2] For him, the private house belonged to the category of

Second Skin. Second edition. Anne Anlin Cheng, Oxford University Press. © Oxford University Press 2023. DOI: 10.1093/oso/9780197748381.003.0005

the useful, not to monumentality; only tombs and public monuments should be considered works of art. But the Baker House represents something of an in-between category: a private house with a healthy dose of monumentality. Not only is the boxy exterior museum-like, but the floor plans within are particularly unusual for a private house (figure 5.2). They, for example, pay extraordinary attention to public spaces even though the design was intended as a domestic residence. The plans delineate several salons and entertainment spaces, conspicuously excluding family life. The kitchen is quite small in relation to the size of the rest of the house.

Yet of all the plans' idiosyncrasies, the most extraordinary feature must be the top-lit, large, double-height (that is, two stories) swimming pool that dominates the center of the house. This swimming pool measures 4 by 9 by 2 meters and would contain about seven tons of water.[3] A magnificent glass roof covers the pool to allow light to fall

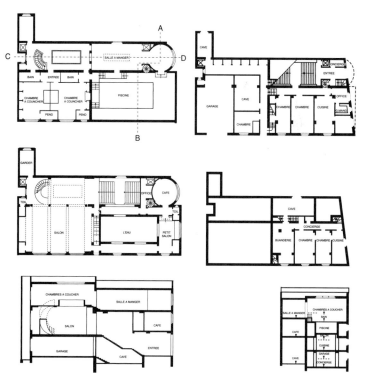

Fig. 5.2

upon the water. The walls of the pool have thick glass windows cut into them, and low passages have been assigned to surround the pool, providing windows onto it, creating for guests of the house something of an "underwater revue" (figure 5.3)[4]

Concealment and theatricality come into full play in this design. And we might think of the water here as playing a similarly critical and ambivalent role to that of the furs in "Lina's Bedroom." If, as I have suggested, Loos was interested in architecture as a kind of maternal covering for the body, an architecture of the womb, then here both ideas are realized, but with a twist. In the Baker House, the inside is made outside, and the trope of the womb becomes hypostatized as the swimming pool in the middle of the house. But the inhabitant of the house (that is, Baker), instead of being the subject securely enclosed, is the object of the gaze. Loos's usual emphasis on the primacy of interiority, instead of offering comfort and covering, here translates into theatricality and exposure. Indeed, the whole house is about entertainment—not Baker's entertainment but the entertainment that is Baker. The guests would come to look at Baker, while she, were she to swim in that pool (that "transparent bowl of water"),[5] would most likely not be able to see the people looking at her because

Fig. 5.3
. . otters in the tide lash, in the kelp-drench, mammal warmth and the inhuman element.

—*Robert Hass*

of the blinding reflections from the top-lit vestibules on the water's surface.

More than realizing a theatrical idiom, the Baker House reproduces a downright peep show. This architectural vision may and has often been said to exemplify the racial and sexual fantasies of European, masculinist, and primitivist desire. We may go even further and see this house as an architectural translation of the banana skirt. For we have traveled from the idea of cloth as the primary instance of architecture, offering cover or shelter, to the banana skirt that offers neither but becomes literalized as architecture in Loos's vision of Baker literally living inside an exposing costume.

Our reading, however, should not stop here. Does this house/water bowl in fact wish to *contain* Baker, and in what sense? What, after all, does it mean to be accused of exposing a subject whose art is exposure itself? When we situate this design in relation to the body of Loos's larger theoretical works on the one hand and Baker's theatrical idiom on the other, we see that this design has much more to tell us about the complications invoked by the politics of specularity and embodiment at the intersection of race and sex. To begin with, we should make the broad observation that although this project is well known in architectural history, only relatively recently have its racial and gender ideologies come under substantial scrutiny. Recent scholarship has traced, from different vantage points, Loos's ideological investment in the masculinization of architecture and this particular design's fantasies about animalized femininity in the service of that interest.[6] The possibility of Loos's masculinist and primitivist desires, therefore, needs no reiteration. But these fantasies should not blind us both to the complications that they generate (for both the dreamer and the dreamed) and to the potential presence of other ghosts in the machine. To see the Baker House as solely a "prurient setting" for masculinist and imperial desire is to miss the fundamental struggle with and intimacy between modernity and nostalgia that structures the very relationship between Black skin and modern surface that we have been following.[7] When we place this design in the larger context of Loos's ongoing ambivalence about "cladding" and Baker's own aesthetic strategy, it becomes clear that multiple and warring desires are being played out in the interior/interiority of the Baker House and that the very subject and the object of this design remain ambiguous. Thus before we can dismiss the Baker House as yet another colonial fantasy, we need to pay attention to the ways in which it may be already enacting erasures of its own.

Let us recall that for Loos, structural solidity is always already a fantasized integrity whose surface is at once organic and prosthetic to that which it contains. By locating the originary desire of architecture in the incipient forms of itinerant surfaces and by narrating architectural history as the departure from that origin, Loosian theory sutures the body to, even as it separates that body from, its encasing—be it stone, cloth, or the skin of the other. In short, in the Loosian narrative of architectural development, the desire to *house* the body grows most vitally out of the desire to *be* the body. Given these slippage between the encasing body and the encased body in Loos's theoretical meditations, it is difficult to say, when it comes to the Baker House, whether the viewing subject in the Baker House is enclosed or enclosing, invading or invaded. As we noted earlier, Loosian interiors have a theatrical inclination and tend to turn everyone who walks through them into part of a view.

Looking at the floor plans of the Baker House, we notice that the guests' views of Baker in the house are constricted and fastidiously managed through devices such as narrow passageways, strategic windows, and segregated layers of glass, turning the theater box very specifically into the peephole even as it transforms the voyeuristic master into the mouse caught in the maze (figure 5.4). There is a mildly claustrophobic tendency in Loos, who once said that "the smallness of a theater box would be unbearable if one could not look out into the large space beyond."[8] Here, in the Baker House, the potential claustrophobic effects of the theater box can only be heightened, rather than relieved, by the claustrophobia of the enclosed indoor swimming pool. That is, both the imaginary Baker and the imaginary guests are potentially enclosed and trapped by this house.

The low external windows, behind the pool gazer, lining the opposite walls of these passageways, have the effect of turning the guest himself or herself into a prospective object of the gaze, highlighting the box-within-box effect of the design. Moreover, by throwing the guest-observer's own reflection back against the glass view onto the

Fig. 5.4
Before it becomes a setting that contains objects, space is not
differentiated from the objects that occupy it.
—*Didier Anzieu*

pool, the design confronts the guest-observer with "his" own reflection, now superimposed against or next to the swimmer (that is, the imaginary Baker). The object status of the viewing subject himself is therefore not just suggested but insisted upon as an inevitable *effect* of looking. In short, the wall of glass operates as medium, barrier, and mirror—indeed, highlighting the constant tension among these terms.

The architectural realization of this apparently fetishistic, masculine vision thus maps out a vertiginous rather than stable relationship between subject and object. Given the crucial yet ambivalent status of "walls" in Loosian theory—either as afterthought or as the very instantiation of cladding—this interior made of layered walls and glass can be understood not as just another theater of display and voyeurism but also as a drama about their restless inversions. It suggests the pliability of body boundaries. Loosian cladding, as an extension of skin, opens and extends the body's boundary into the exterior world, rendering that body at once imperial and porous. For Loos, the disavowed primal scene of architecture is the revelation of the transferable and inchoative nature of structure itself. And it is precisely the reactivation and repetition of this primal element that turns Loos's structural efforts to contain Baker into something less stable than one would suppose.

As Beatriz Colomina has astutely pointed out, the swimmer in the tank, while most likely blinded to the spectators outside the pool, nonetheless would see her own reflection in the glass—that is, she would be not simply an object of gaze but also an object for herself.[9] Thus, the voyeuristic is layered over by the narcissistic. Building on Colomina's insight, let us extend a similar doubleness to the voyeur himself. Imagine Loos imagining himself standing by the glass pool and enclosed by the corridor, looking into the water that also reflects him and extends well over his head, feeling the walls behind him and the windows that in turn frame him. Who, then, is the supposed object or subject of this design? Just as "Lina's Bedroom" discloses a fantasy of envelopment that implicates Loos as much as the Lina of his imagination, so must we see the very entrance into the Baker House (by owner, guest, and architect alike) as an entry into a world of relentless and indiscriminate visibility that affects viewer as well as the viewed, male as well as female subjects.

In their influential essay "Transparency: Literal and Phenomenal," Colin Rowe and Robert Slutsky distinguish material transparency (matter that one can see through) from structural transparency (a phenomenological condition in which one can see different planes, both temporal and spatial, simultaneously). Here this "transparent bowl" of water proves itself to be structurally rather than materially transparent. Moreover, we can see the Loosian window onto the pool as also a mirror through which one sees the simultaneity of one's self and the other.[10] The glass view onto Baker thus gestures to identificatory longing as well as desire. The desire *to have* and the desire *to be* merge, rendering the glass and the watery skin of Baker as phenomenally transparent surfaces, at once within and without the subject, an object of nostalgia and inexorable separation. In short, if Loos's design is meant to expose Baker's skin, we have to wonder if it also reveals his desire *to be in that skin*. What it means to occupy space thus comes very close to what it means to be occupied. We are in fact confronting an implicit critique of modern architecture as monumentality and its implied project of self-mastery. For if one narrative about modern architecture is that it enacts temporal resistance, that is, modern architecture responds to modernity's acceleration and change by forging an idealist aesthetics as a means of battling the caprice of time and fashion, then Loos's own productions of "feminine" and "racialized" surfaces—fur, finely grained marble, water—actually write against such conservation.

Just as attention to Loos's own theories complicates the scopic mastery implied in the Baker House, so do Baker's theatrical methods forge a counterlens through which to reconsider the apparent relationship between seeing and being seen staged by this architectural design. We cannot address the politics of specularity in this house without also taking into consideration the politics of looking that the figure of Baker already embodies and troubles, for Baker's own mode of exhibitionism might very well reorganize (or recode) the specular exchange embedded in the Baker House.

So what exactly is the nature of Baker's exhibitionism? We know that Baker's theatrical idiom (with its multiple and persistent modes of staged nakedness) is heavily reliant on the trope of the peep show, on the structural opposition between inside and outside. It is, after all, the mise-en-scène of this dichotomy that normally allows any striptease to be effective. Yet contrary to this expectation, Baker's particular brand of exhibitionism actually relies on the layered conflation of concealment and exposure, of essence and performance, of flesh and skin. Indeed, Baker's famous nakedness begins to look less and less apparent upon close analysis. When one looks at her "nudity," what one finds is not what one expects. She was known for exploiting her nudity,[11] but key moments of exposure in her films and photographs often involve elaborate engagement with both literal and symbolic veils. It turns out that this "fugitive" (as French critic Pierre de Régnier called Baker) is an escape artist, one who is particularly good at outrunning scopic regimes. In her first feature film, *La sirène des tropiques* (directed by Henri Etievant, 1927), where Baker plays Papitou, the biracial daughter of an "old colonialist," we find an exquisite example of how the exposure of Baker relies contradictorily on the covering up of Baker.

Although *La sirène des tropiques* does offer us a quick, obligatory scene of the-half-naked-native-girl-caught-by-the-stream-by-her-white-landlord, the film is much more memorable for its extended sequence of hide-and-seek in which Papitou, having stowed away on an ocean liner, leads the ship's guests and crew on a wild chase. The question of Papitou's visibility—literally, "can you see her?"—is accompanied by an elaborate process of visual layering; that is, the entire sequence is about piling surface after surface on Papitou/Baker. First, Papitou dives into the brown water wearing a typical late-Victorian dress of white muslin. When she climbs on board, the potential "wet-shirt" scenario is discarded in favor of the opposite: Baker's clinging dress is in fact covered by muck and tendrils from the sea. Once on board, wherever she goes, she leaves a telltale trail of muddy prints; yet her body manages to escape detection again and again. She then falls into the coal bin in the boiler room, completely covering herself in an opaque blackness that announces its superficiality against her natural skin. This darkening of Papitou's skin enacts both revelation (symbolizing her filth and primitiveness) and camouflage (allowing her to hide undetected in dark corners). If "blackness" in this scene is ambivalent, then it becomes even more mysterious in its ability to take to its supposed opposite, that is, whiteness. For the coal-covered Papitou then proceeds to hide herself in an oversized flour bin, succeeding in dousing herself from head to toe in white flour. This "racial" conversion happens immediately after a frightened guest has exclaimed, "She's easy to recognize. She's all black!"—as if underscoring precisely the unreliability of presumed racial legibility.

There are at least two jokes here about visual legibility: first, a comment about the superficial nature of stardom (Baker's recognizability), and second, the flirtation with the idea of race-as-surface that can be added on or taken off. In this sequence, is Papitou seeable or a figment of someone's imagination? A person or a shadow that flits by the corner of one's eyes? Her body emerges and disappears in a mischievous relay between dark and light, between materiality and stealth. Papitou's flight does not come to an end until she decides to scrub herself clean in the tub of a stateroom into which she has stolen. She is discovered there, trespassing and *déshabillée*, as if only the evidence of her "real," naked, and illicit body might arrest the dizzying inversions of colors on her body and assure the diegetic spectator of the recognizability/

locatability of the Black body in the end. Yet even as the colonial ideology driving the plot labors to assimilate this sequence as a symbolic dirtying and then baptism of the Black body (the diegesis is, after all, all about disciplining Papitou into the rewards of self-sacrifice), what remains harder to erase is the memory of Papitou's sartorial antics and the haunting possibility that the "natural" state of the naked Black body may be all about covers. Moreover, her assumptions of these covers and the subsequent play they allowed between being phantom and corporeal, between shadow and weight, suggest a delight in the pleasures and privileges of a fractured or doubled subjectivity. What does it mean to have and to assume a body that does *not* crumble when objectified and made to disappear? This body does not retain its integrity by consolidating itself; it does so by dissimulating and disseminating itself.

Seen in this light, Baker as performer may bear more affinity to contemporary performance artists such as Sophie Calle, Angelika Festa, and Lorna Simpson than we would have guessed, all of whom respond to the potential traps of female visuality and commodification by dynamically playing with appearance and disappearance. Indeed, the tension between presence and absence generates the central energy behind Baker's famous corporeality. Oscar Wilde once quipped that "the true mystery of the world is the visible, not the invisible,"[12] and nowhere is this counterintuitive insight more pronounced than in the climactic scene of the French film *Princesse Tam Tam* (directed by Edmond T. Gréville, 1935), starring Baker. This Pygmalion plot tells the story of a Frenchman, Max de Mirecourt (Albert Préjean), who imports from Tunisia a street urchin named Alwina (Baker), whom he "civilizes" to pass her off as African royalty to Parisian society. In the climax of the plot, Max brings his fake African princess to a popular Parisian nightclub to show her off (and to test her) as a culmination of his pedagogical achievement. At the beginning of this scene, Alwina enters the club on Max's arm, clad in a fluid gown of gold lamé—an art deco dream epitomizing the refinement of civilization (figure 5.5).

Life is a luminous halo, indeed. But while Max is not looking, his wife, Lucie (the competing "light," played by Germaine Aussey), conspires with her society cronies to ply Alwina with alcohol and to persuade her to dance to the so-called jungle music, also arranged by Lucie. According to the plot, Alwina cannot resist the call of the wild

Fig. 5.5
She enters through a dense electric twilight.
—*E. E. Cummings*

and is tricked into making a spectacle of herself when she jumps from her chair and runs to the top of the baroque stage's central spiral staircase. From there, she descends in a rush of physical pleasure, all the while stripping off her golden French designer gown. She then proceeds to dance with abandon on the ground stage in her inimitable style.

This, then, is the famous strip scene from *Princesse Tam Tam*. Yet this scene of literal and symbolic "outing" is bizarre in more ways than one. What exactly is it that is being exposed? Given that Alwina's "true color"—that is, her racial color—has never been a secret in the story, it cannot be the literalness of her Blackness that so shocks the Parisian audience. We may say, of course, that what has been uncovered is precisely the nonliteral nature of racial difference. This account would go something like this: while the diegetic audience may know the princess to be Black, it has not known how Black until now. So Alwina may be able to pass as a princess for a while, but her wild African nature will invariably reveal itself. In this account, we are reminded that class is not enough to overcome racial difference.

Still, this explanation does not fully address the peculiarities of the scene. There is much in this scene of exhibitionism to suggest that what you see is not what you get. For one thing, this catastrophic dance, so dependent on notions of visibility and disclosure, oddly enough effects a series of visual confusions, even occlusions. Cinematographically, the sequence is shot in a series of quick jump cuts that literally make it difficult to see. Cutting into Alwina's number are shots of a host of other subjects: the orchestra, dancers from the chorus, the white male and female audience, even segments that look more like spliced-in footage than a properly diegetic scene. The whole produces a kind of visual proliferation and equivalences in this vibrating number. In fact, there is a sequence within this scene in which the viewer sees nothing but a kaleidoscopic series of indiscriminate, truncated, dancing body parts. We are given entangled and writhing hands, arms, legs, and feet that belong to everyone and to no one. So if Alwina is being displayed as an object of fetishistic voyeurism, then it is curiously nonspecific and prolific. Racial difference, we are told, is highly dependent on visual availability and legibility. Yet here what it means to discern, identify, and recognize someone becomes exquisitely problematic precisely at the *site/sight* of the visible.

The fetish, often cited as a particularly ocular fantasy (the shine on the nose, for example), engenders in fact a crisis of seeing. In this context, we see why the mythical figure Sigmund Freud associates with fetishism was the figure of the blinding Medusa. For if the scene of Baker's unwitting exhibition is all about revelation and the European audience's prurient intake of that visual exposé, it is also a scene about the *impossibility of looking at the visible.* The fact is, in this "striptease," nothing has been shown. Anyone who has seen the film would remember that Alwina strips off her gold lamé gown only to reveal *another* dress. Thanks to the magic of cinematography, a full-length black gown manages miraculously to exist underneath the body-hugging sheath of gold. Thus, in lieu of skin, we get cloth. In other words, the deflecting "shine" of the fetish has been removed only to reveal not the ghastly gap of castration but the smoothness of yet another seamless surface. If part of the illusion of colonial imperialism is the fantasy of penetrating a territory-as-body, then here in this striptease the body offers itself not as depth or flesh but as mobile outline or, at the most, another costume. Theatricalized Black female skin, like its corollary modern building surface, acts as a surrogate, the perfect supplement to a missing body.

Baker constantly gives us surface rather than body. Even in her most "embodied" dances, it can be argued that it is her kinesthetic energy rather than her corporeal presence that transmits. Here in *Princesse Tam Tam*, instead of unveiled skin, the viewer gets only the movements of unraveling skein, an unraveling, furthermore, that is particularly unrevealing. If Baker's persona has been overwhelmingly invested in the idea of the materiality of her physical body, then we have to add that there has also been an equal inclination to subject that body to, as well as for that body to insist upon its own, abstraction.

The *metaphor* of bare/visible skin comes to stand in for the assured materiality of exposed flesh. We are forcibly reminded that the idea (indeed, redundancy) of "bare skin" is itself always tropologically produced. In a sense, this is also the very paradox structuring almost all modes of racial identification: *an avowal of physical difference that is in fact deeply metaphysical and abstract.* And it is this paradox that Baker's acts of "stripping" repeatedly enact rather than assuage. If anything, it is the lack of "real skin" that renders this scene truly obscene for the colonial gaze. In the film, among the rubbernecking crowd, we see the two people who find it difficult to look: Max and his co-conspirator in the ruse. Here the master puppeteers wince, turn their faces away, and shield their eyes from the spectacle before them. The plot will have us believe that these two French men cannot bear the exposure of their scheme. Critics will tell us that they cannot bear the depth of Alwina's "true" Blackness. I propose, instead, that what these men cannot bear to witness is not Alwina's Blackness but its failure. More precisely, it is Blackness's failure to provide distinction: the horrifying insight that *the "glittery" and the "blackened" may be uncannily equivalent.* The essence of Africa supposedly revealed in this scene, to be contrasted against authentic Frenchness implied by the plot, comes down finally to a costume change. It is Max and his buddy who come closest to being confronted by the emptiness behind the colonial fetish: a lack that determines not only the object but also the subject of colonial desire.[13]

Going back, then, to that specular swimming tank in the Baker House, we begin to see how that design may not contain or capture Baker at all but is instead *already a reading of her disappearance*. It provides an architectural instantiation of her theatrical method: the staging of a spectacle through which the subject escapes, a paradoxical structure of exposed and layered surfaces that vertiginously reverts view and viewer, that turns what is inside into outside and vice versa. If Baker's theatricalized nakedness offers a complex business about how difficult it is to be naked, then so does the interior of this house, designed to showcase this famous woman, embody a crisis about seeing—more accurately, a crisis about the mastery of seeing.

Psychoanalyst and cultural theorist Darian Leader reminds us, "When we desire in the visual field, we expect that the object of our desires remains just that, an object."[14] As he points out, a lot can happen to disrupt that complacency. The object can look back and show itself to be desiring. Or, in our case, mirrorlike, that object can reflect back on us the precariousness of our own subjectivity. That was what potentially threatened Picasso in the Trocadéro and Loos in front of that tank of water. It is perhaps not mere irony that the Baker House, so well known in architectural historiography, is itself an object of hide-and-seek when it comes to its place in Baker biography. Baker herself never wrote about the project, neither its consignment nor its reception. Biographers do mention the project but usually as just one example in a string of tributes made to Baker during her lifetime by famous men. It is often assumed that Baker did not choose to build the house because she would not want to live in such a reputedly primitive and exposing house.[15] Biographers and critics have observed that Baker may have suffered from a shyness belied by her publicity and that her famous comedic style—her trademark eye- and knee-crossing, for instance—could very well serve as a defensive mechanism to deflect the intense erotic attentions so often focused on her.[16]

At the same time, we know that this is a woman who was extraordinarily accomplished at and prone to self-image making. From the life-size wax diorama of her (named "Jorama") at Château des Milandes in Dordogne, to the outdoor artificial lily pond in which she swam naked at her Parisian suburban residence Le Beau Chêne in Le Vésinet, to the vast archive of photographic, filmic, and artistic images for which she posed, to her trademark nudity onstage and in film, Baker knew how to specularize herself better and in more media than any other entertainer of her time, or even ours.[17] Baker clearly grasped, if not helped to shape, the underlying structure of modern celebrity. (Walt Disney, Madonna, and Michael Jackson have nothing on Baker when it comes to the machinery of image making!) Both Des Milandes and Le Beau Chêne—with successive rooms effusively layered and decorated with publicity photos, postcards, brochures, and wax exhibits—were elaborate museums and open to the public while they were still her residences. So which is the real Baker, the shy woman or the publicity hound?

Perhaps we might understand these choices not as alternatives but as two sides of one method: that of impersonation. That is to say, Baker is expertly skilled at *making models of herself*, which both shield and reveal her. In short, she wears her nudity—and her images—like second skins. When placed in specific relation to Baker's own theatrical strategy, the Baker House then begins to suggest not so much exploitation as simulation. A twin to Loos's own architectural impersonations, Baker as performer suggests that perhaps what might have given her pause about this house may have been not its exploitation but its imitation of her. The specular dynamics of the Baker House begin to look less like an inscription *about* Baker than an inscription that aims to be *like* Baker.

The surface (or skin/dress) of the house enacts a similar, complex game of hide-and-seek. The trouble of seeing—and of segregating subjectivity from objectivity, of differentiating transparency from opacity—that we experienced inside is redoubled on the hypnotic facade of alternating, contrasting bands (each 30 centimeters wide) of black and white marble. In architectural literature, this striking facade has repeatedly been described as "tattooed" or erotically marked.[18] This rather idiosyncratic designation only makes sense when one understands it as a deliberate allusion to Loos's own references to tattoos, with the implication that Loos, in designing for the "primitive" Baker, has lapsed into the very ornamentation that he abhors. Indeed, numerous commentaries about the Baker House have found this design to be unusual in Loos's repertoire and have repeatedly described it without much critical reflection as "primitive," "exotic," or "African."[19] The claim suggests that the surface of the Baker House, instead of being blank, is markedly decorated and attention-drawing, hence feminized and regressive. The black-and-white pattern, also thought to mimic zebra stripes, a popularized and stylized primitivist motif, has thus been universally understood as typifying "colonial spaces" with all the concomitant masculine and imperial ideologies.

At the same time, however, when we reexamine the Baker House facade, we can just as reasonably claim that it is significantly *not* tattooed. The smooth marble bears no marking, and the material's traditionally assumed nobility can also be said to resist even as it historically embodies primitive aesthetics. The black and white colors, ingrained into the load-bearing marble, are decorative but not ornamental in the applied sense. Are we seeing ornament or cladding? And are we seeing black on white or white on black? In fact, the very process by which we discern negative from positive space becomes vertiginous. The so-called tattooed exterior articulates a grammar of recursion and proximity rather than one of hierarchy. Is this striking facade a colonial prison or a masquerade?

The engagement with the "primitive" in the Baker House is instructive, not at the level of how it labels Baker but at the level of what it tells us about Loos's—and, by extension, modernism's—Janus-faced aesthetics. The evaluation of the Baker House facade as unusually and erotically marked and unlike any of Loos's other projects is, in fact, not accurate. Loos's choice of contrasting black and white marble (in various geometric incarnations) is in accordance with several designs in his repertoire. Loos deploys variants of black-and-white patterns in both exterior and interior usage in projects such as American Bar (or the Kärntner Bar, 1908; figure 5.6); the Goldman Salatsch House (1911; figure 5.7); the Villa Karma (1904–1906; figures 5.8–5.10); the Steiner Store (1907); the Manz Store (1912); and the Knize Salon (1913)—none of which, by the way, got read as "tattooed."[20]

Given this recurring motif in Loos's work, to call the black-and-white Baker House a singularly tattooed building bearing a primitivist inscription is to have but performed an inscription about its client.

The recurring black and white marble stripes in fact partake of Loos's larger, ongoing interest in Moorish architectural design dating from the ninth century that resurfaced in Western Europe and applied most notably in Italy and Spain. The Duomo in Siena—more specifically its campanile—represents one of the most memorable examples

Fig. 5.6
The American Bar, 1908

of the use of black and white stripes.[21] This tells us again, from another perspective, how Loos's modernist buildings are as nostalgic as they are forward-looking. This also alerts us to the complexity of the function of these stripes once Loos chooses to apply them to the Baker House.

On the one hand, the stripes (gesturing to either zebras or dark Moorish bodies) lead us directly to a network of expected associations among animality, primitivism, and criminality rehearsed well into the nineteenth century. We recall that Loos labels ornamentation—and, in particular, the tattoo—as criminal. For Loos, criminality signifies specifically a breach against civilization, progress, and the efficiency of mechanical production. Thus, while the primitive man decorates himself out of ontological or spiritual needs, according to Loos, the

Fig. 5.7
Goldman Salatsch House, 1911

civilized man should not need to, since he has sufficient modes of sub-
limation and production at his disposal to render such atavistic desires
superfluous and self-indulgent:

> Man had progressed far enough for ornament to no longer produce
> erotic sensations in him, unlike the Papuans, a tattooed face did not
> increase the aesthetic value, but reduced it. Man had progressed far
> enough to find pleasure in purchasing a plain cigarette case, even if it
> cost the same as the one that was ornamented.[22]

Consequently, erotic and hence nonutilitarian ornamentation on the
part of the modern man signals his innate degeneracy:

Fig. 5.8
Villa Karma, dining room, 1904–1906

The modern man who tattoos himself is a criminal or degenerate. There are prisons where eighty percent of the inmates bear tattoos.... If a tattooed person dies at liberty, it is only that he died a few years before he committed a murder. [23]

The anatomist-craniometrician Cesare Lombroso famously calls the criminal an "atavistic being who reproduces in his person the ferocious instincts of primitive humanity and the inferior animal."[24] The traditional nineteenth-century use of zebra stripes in standard prison uniforms in Britain and America, for instance, was considered not only practical in hindering escape but also useful as a means of marking shame, a gesture of humiliation meant to invoke notions of innate degeneracy on the part of the criminal (figure 5.11).[25]

Fig. 5.9
Villa Karma, front entrance, 1904–1906

The notion of criminality is thus deeply tied to ideals of modern society and the civilization that it enforces, and the striped pattern connotes the outward signs of both primitive degeneracy and its enslavement/bondage by civil law.

On the other hand, sublimations have the unfortunate tendency to announce or reenact the very desires that they purport to defuse. Just as the very idea of a "cigarette case" (even a plain one) as an extraneous case designed to both cover over and showcase an oral attachment is itself already a sign of civilization's enduring erotic expressions, so do the zebra stripes finally embody the continuity, rather than the opposition, between criminality and civilization, between brute animality and refined humanity. The motif of the zebra stripe, a stylistic synecdoche for

Fig. 5.10
Villa Karma, skylight, 1904–1906

animal skin itself, surprisingly, *also* draws from the ideal of abstract mechanization and its implicit celebration of ideal humanity. That is, the zebra stripes also typify the regularized, repetitive, geometric pattern of the machine age.

It is worth remembering that in the early twentieth century, the standardization required by mechanical reproduction, rather than being thought of as antihumanist or a threat, was seen to reconcile modernity with classical humanism. Think of Walter Gropius's campaign for standardization and anonymous collectivity in the '30s, as well as the new functionalism that revolutionized the fashion industry at the turn of the century. This is also the ideological backdrop for what J. C. Flugel in 1930 calls modern men's renunciation of style, paving the road for the popularization of uniform clothing that serves as the ideological foundations

Fig. 5.11
The invention of the modern criminal cannot be disassociated from the
construction of a law-abiding body.
—*Allan Seluka*

for commercial ventures such as the Banana Republics of today. (Indeed,
Banana Republic, as both retail and aesthetic practice, may be seen as a
direct continuation of the entwined histories of imperialism and democracy to which Baker and her banana skirt were already gesturing half
a century earlier.)[26] It is more than ironic and in fact historically consistent that the passionate, violent battles over bananas in the modern
age—fought in courtrooms, in boardrooms, on foreign soils, over Black
bodies, and impacting international politics—have these days mostly
receded from public memory to reemerge as the most docile of traces: in
the studiously cultivated taste of democratic fashion.

   In the early half of the twentieth century, abstract geometric
patterns, like the black-and-white pattern under our consideration
here, thus may be said to provide the stylistic expression of an ideal
that combines standardized mechanics with human harmony. In fact,

contrasting and geometric stripes were often deployed as signs of modernity and progress in both architectural projects and popular culture from the 1920s through the '50s. From the 1930s through the '50s, the famous Manhattan nightclub El Morocco would signal its exoticism and its modernity through its signature decor of blue zebra stripes. The modern bathing suits from the early 1920s—as part of the new streamlined activewear—often sported a similar pattern (figure 5.12).

Fig. 5.12
How to take advantage of these new freedoms?
—*Le Corbusier*

In 1940, director Howard Hawks would dress his version of the New Woman, played by Rosalind Russell in *His Girl Friday* (a remake of *The Front Page*, 1931, directed by Lewis Milestone), in a striking, almost dizzying geometric suit of black and white stripes (figure 5.13).

It is worth mentioning, for fans of Hildy Johnson, the character played by Russell, that this female protagonist is very much the modern woman caught in the vexingly identical pulls of bondage and freedom. Her striped suit, representing style and independence, will come to echo the prison cell encasing the condemned prisoner Earl Williams, whom she tries to save and who, of course, offers a double for Hildy herself.

Loos himself in the projects mentioned earlier deploys black-and-white patterns as signs of stark simplicity in direct refutation of Viennese opulence. In this way, the zebra pattern may be said to represent, rather than contrast with, the very ideal of modernist abstraction. But now, in the light of our discussion, we have to add a third term: that this harmony between machine and man in fact turns on the necessary and mediating presence of the animal/zebra (and, I would suggest,

Fig. 5.13
The finest achievement of the new woman has been personal liberty.
—*Winnifred Harper Cooley*

racialized and feminized other).[27] It is not that the zebra pattern could connote the animal as well as the mechanical but that these categories *speak through one another*: a synchronicity. Thus, the use of black-and-white patterns in Loos's work signifies simultaneously the simplicity of modernity and the ornamentalness of Moorish antiquity. Let us be explicit. Why do the first modern bathing suits look like prisoners' outfits? Because the possibility of a modern, newly liberated, streamlined body, facilitated by innovations in synthetic textile fibers that act like a second skin on the flesh, is an *extension of,* not an antithesis to, the idea of the atavistic, unruly, mobile body born out of primitivized animality.

Returning to the striped facade of the Baker House, we begin to see how modernism, machine, animal, and atavistic woman converge on its very surface, demonstrating not oppositions but a philosophic continuity. The animal, the human, and the mechanical—the three foundational, distinctive categories that underpin modernism—turn out to provide the preconditions for each other's discretion, a series of disavowals that are, however, perfectly announced on the surface. In short, the categories of the animal, the human, and the machine, while ideologically segregated, are stylistically identical. It is at the level of style—the most apparent of styles (though hidden in its very transparency)—that we can witness the profound contact between modernism and its others. It is also here that we begin to see the fashioning behind the making of the primitive body and of the modern structure. The denuding of both relies on tropological effects.

To put it another way, what the Baker portrayal of naked, racialized femininity shares with the facade of the Baker House in the end is not only the ambivalent vocabulary of primitivism but also the historic, social, aesthetic, and philosophical problem of how to fashion skin/surface, how to naturalize that which has been—can only be—fundamentally tailored or stylized. The "skin" of the Baker House reveals that there is no such thing as a naked house, just as there can never be a truly naked body. When it comes to the racialized body, the literal is always metaphorically manufactured, even as that fabrication bears a literalness of its own. We are, in other words, looking at the material traces of the metaphorical. Or, to put it less aphoristically and more exactly, we are recovering the literal residue of a racial logic that operates allegorically.

Finally, if the Baker House is meant to provide a "dress" for Baker, might we not consider how it is also fashioning a dress for Loos himself? Not surprisingly, in addition to buildings, Loos was vitally interested in fashion. An active advocate for the Reform Dress Movement and the new freedom of the body, Loos argues in his 1902 essay "Ladies' Fashion" for the shedding of excessive clothing for women and that the modern woman should no longer submit to the lures of "velvet and silk, flowers and ribbons, feathers and paints."[28] This is in fact the same argument he makes for modern men. Here he will first formulate the terms that will be fully developed six years later in "Ornament and Crime":

> Ornament is something that must be overcome. The Papuan and the criminal ornament their skin. The Indian covers his paddle and his boat with layers and layers of ornament. But the bicycle and the steam engine are free of ornament. The march of civilization systematically liberates object after object from ornamentation.[29]

Within the larger context of Loos's writing, we are more than aware of the fragility underlying the insistent separation of mechanization from atavism, masculinity from femininity, and objects from subjects. Surely we hear the fervent declaration that ornament "must be overcome" as much as an injunction to himself as to his female audience, just as we know that in the larger discourse of modernism, "bicycles and steam engines" are hardly free from the burdens of human longings (figure 15.14).

With the sleek marble surface of the Baker House, it is as if Loos denudes Baker (of her feathers and paints) in order to modernize rather than to primitivize her, but to say so is also to acknowledge the possibility that he is also dressing her (and himself) in the very nude facade that is profoundly nostalgic for the cover of borrowed skins. If the facade of the Baker House is at all tattooed, it is marked not by the inscription of masculinist desire but by the traces of its struggles, perhaps even its relinquishment. It is on the surface of the Baker House that Loos's lifelong conflict between the call of cladding versus ornamentation, between masculinized architecture and feminized/primitive sensuality, comes to its most striking articulation.

In the end, it may not be the irrefutable materiality of Baker's skin that draws Loos but precisely its affinities for portable covers. In other words, the Baker "body" that haunts Loos and his conceptualizations of modern buildings may be not primarily its eroticized flesh but its infinitely dressable surface. Around the same time that Loos was designing his house for Baker, a photograph of the performer was taken in Paris.

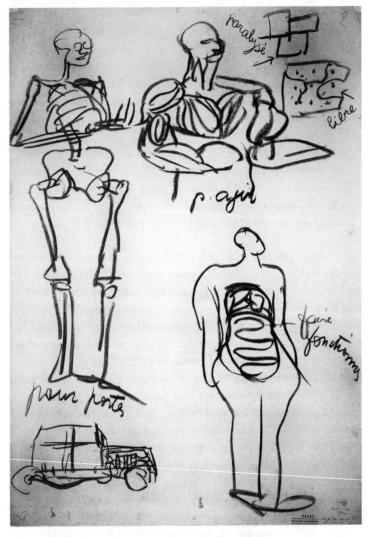

Fig. 5.14
this skeleton for carrying
this muscular filling *for action*
these viscera *to feed and to operate* . . .
a frame
a body
a motor with its organs.
—*Le Corbusier*

Fig. 5.15

In this image (figure 5.15), Baker sports a dress with a matching coat in a black-and-white abstract zebra pattern. The silhouette of this outfit invokes the ideas behind the reformed "English suit" with its re- laxed lines, cut for the ease of movement. For the French press then and some critics today, this image symbolizes Baker's sophistication and triumph against her jungle image.[30] By now, however, it is impossible for us not to see the complex web of meanings interwoven into the surface (and implied body) of that suit. Indeed, as we have seen, as early as the '20s and '30s, zebra patterns of black and white have come to embody the sign for modern simplicity, bringing in full circle the tautology of civilization and its imagined prehistories.

Did Loos design this house in order to simulate Baker's body, be it in consumption or identification? Or has that already simulated body preempted the house by wearing it?

6

Radiant Bodies, Dark Cities

Manhattan—I'm up a tree. . . .
With a million neon rainbows burning below me
And a million blazing taxis raising a roar
Here I sit, above the town
In my pet pailletted gown
Down in the depths on the ninetieth floor.
While the crowds at El Morocco punish the parquet
And at "21" the couples clamor for more,
I'm deserted and depressed
In my regal eagle nest
Down in the depths on the ninetieth floor. . . .
　　　—"Down in the Depths (On the Ninetieth Floor),"
　　　　　　　　　　　　　　　　Cole Porter, 1936

At the height of Josephine Baker's early career in Europe, a songwriter
from Peru, Indiana, who became an international icon in his own right
wrote a song called "Down in the Depths (On the Ninetieth Floor)." A
blues song riding on a light tune, Cole Porter's lyrics balance a series
of tensile opposites—height and depth, throng and desolation, privilege and exclusion, embodiment and disembodiment—that simultaneously carry spatial, social, and psychological dimensions. (We also
find, by the way, the reappearance of those ubiquitous zebra stripes,
this time invoked by the reference to El Morocco, the well-known
Manhattan nightclub from the '20s through the '40s famous for its
zebra-striped banquettes and contrasting parquet floors.)[1] In the infrastructure of Porter's modern city, or what Ann Douglas has more
intriguingly called "mongrel Manhattan," the exotic and the modern
converge, blending elements of the human, the technological, and the

Second Skin. Second edition. Anne Anlin Cheng, Oxford University Press. © Oxford University Press 2023.
DOI: 10.1093/oso/9780197748381.003.0006

animal. And in the heart of this hybrid landscape stands the high-rise, which signals more starkly than any other material symbols the height of American technological ingenuity.

More than testifying to modern technological advancement, the skyscraper also exemplifies the dream of a brand-new form of living and subjectivity. The skyscraper's impenetrable surface (or, at least, it seemed so back at the dawn of twentieth-century America) and its anonymity were originally meant not to alienate the modern subject but to protect him or her from the onslaught of modern life (or, in the *King Kong* fantasy, the onslaught of violent savagery). Yet as the architectural instantiation of the psychological state of being "blasé" that Georg Simmel diagnosed as the modern condition, skyscraper living also carries with it the ache of modernism.[2] At once shelter and trap, the skyscraper is both a product of industrialization and an embodiment of the subsequent anxiety about the illogics of that industrial society. It stands as a tribute to modern technology and as a symbol of human hubris (the pillar that connects the earth to heaven), but it also expresses an anxiety about the limits of the human body. The skyscraper thus aims to extend, or even serve as a prosthetic for, the frail and bounded human body. Indeed, the technological innovation and structural design of the skyscraper echo this bodily greed: a growable, self-carrying steel skeleton, covered over with curtains of concrete that are often described as "skin."[3]

If technological invention aims to mime or extend the human, the inverse is always a haunting possibility, for not only does the skyscraper offer both protection and isolation, but Porter's lyrics also suggest that it may even incite in its occupants an invidious desire. The human body may begin to long for a similarly impervious existence. And here we come at last to the one human figure in this song: Porter's world-weary heroine. (Dare we ask, is she Black or white, female or fugitive?) This woman is birdlike, specifically a large bird of prey, recalling the ancient association between birds and women so favored by Sigmund Freud.[4] But this woman is not just human and animal. Encased in one of the most striking emblems of Western, masculinist, industrial power, she is also machinelike. Even her gown simulates the skyscraper itself: a cover that simultaneously protects and imprisons the body that it sheathes. Indeed, that dress comes to personify, almost literally, the morphological mutation between steel and skin: "Here I sit, above the town, / In my pet pailletted gown."[5] At once impenetrable and vulnerable, Porter's heroine in the sky embodies the fusion or reflection of the structural and the ontological. The spangle-encrusted fabric that envelops her indexes subjectivity *and* its camouflage, gesturing to selfhood and the othering necessary to achieving that integrity.

The animal ("pet") that is the dress and the human that is the body duplicate not only each other but also the very building that houses them. Building, dress, and body appear as distinct structures that are in fact distinctively mimetic of one another. So are we looking at another instance of a building wrapping itself around a woman or the woman wearing the building?

The specter of Baker haunts this song—not only because she is also a diva with a penchant for glittery metallic gowns or because she walks about with her own "pailletted" pet, a leopard named Chiquita that sports a reflective diamond collar and that offers a teasing metaphor for Baker herself—but, most pertinently, because she also invokes the permutation between body and (modern) structure. By now it will not surprise the reader to learn that Baker had an impact not only on Adolf Loos but also on that other well-known father of modern architecture, Le Corbusier. Both Loos and Le Corbusier were entranced by Baker and skyscrapers alike. The connection between these two passions is not as eccentric as it sounds when we remember that both Baker and the skyscraper represent American difference to these men, and America itself enjoys a fantasmatic function in the European imaginary, much in the same way as Africa does. If Africa represents unbridled passion and naivety for Europeans at the turn of the century, then America represents a different but equally exoticized energy, the passions and optimism of a new age of mechanization and industrial democracy. Europeans were captivated by demonstrations of American knowhow, its mechanization and consumption, symbolized by skyscrapers, infrastructure, plumbing, gadgets, and advertising.[6] Both Baker and skyscrapers promise euphoric escape for a world-weary fin-de-siècle Europe. Americanness (*Américanisme* in French and *Amerikanismus* in German) was the other frontier in European primitivism.

More important, both Loos's and Le Corbusier's conceptualizations about architecture, its forms and functions, were deeply influenced by their visits to America and, in particular, by their impressions of American cities. Loos's career really did not take off until after his two-year stay in America, where he worked odd jobs like dishwashing. He was especially enamored of Chicago and New York and their landscape of rising skyscrapers. In 1923, he submitted a well-known proposal for the Chicago Tribune Tower.[7] The American skyscraper with its skeletal steel frame and its thin cladding must have represented for Loos (much like Baker herself) a beautiful metaphor for the possibilities of building as a new prosthetic body—one that is clean, functional, yet also designed to cover and protect man.[8]

Le Corbusier, arguably one of the most influential architects of the twentieth century, was a great fan and critic of American cities such as Chicago and New York. On the one hand, he was enthralled by New York and the skyscraper. Here is Le Corbusier's version of New York to go along with Porter's:

> No one can imagine [Manhattan] who has not seen it. It is a titanic mineral display, a prismatic stratification shot through with an infinite number of lights, from top to bottom, in depth, in a violent silhouette like a fever chart beside a sick bed. A diamond, incalculable diamonds.[9]

On the other hand, America was also a disappointment because it failed to be as modern as Le Corbusier would have liked.[10] Manhattan instantiates, for Le Corbusier, a fervent embodiment of machine, radiance, and animality—a lurking, violent silhouette—that has not quite reached its full potential. This view of Manhattan as at once modern and not quite is in turn rhythmically and thematically related to Le Corbusier's perception about popular American culture, specifically, jazz and the American Black body as entertainment:

> Negro music . . . is the melody of the soul joined with the rhythm of the machine. It is in two-part time; tears in the heart; movement of legs, torso, arms and head. . . . [It was] the sound of modern times.[11]

Now we can easily contextualize Le Corbusier's chain of association connecting modernity, American cityscape, skyscrapers, technology, and jazz as part of the synthesis of folk culture and mechanical forms that characterizes Parisian modernism at large. This familiar summary has produced a general liberal impatience with modernist primitivism and has limited the attention paid to the psychical and philosophical negotiations resulting from that synthesis. That is, given the racist projections and appropriations at work here, need the critic say anything more? Yet, as we have seen with Loos (and Pablo Picasso), it is precisely the complex, unpredictable, and more politically confounding moments between modernist primitivism and the passionate objects of its engagement that may in fact hold the key to unraveling the uncomfortable intimacy between that liberal judgment and the symptom it diagnoses.

In *Quand les cathedrals etaient blanches: Voyage aux pays de timides*, a text written after his brief but intense trip to America in the autumn of 1935, Le Corbusier sought to address his love for and disappointment with New York City. He advocated for a reformed "second machine age" that would promote a demolition-based planning proposal for Manhattan as an empirical model for the ideal city, filled with skyscrapers and row houses, a concept that would be fulfilled in his lecture on his plans "La ville radieuse" (1937).[12] Attempting to confront the problems of the modern city—issues of circulation, population, space, and hygiene—he thus sought to transform Manhattan from what he perceived as an "enchanted catastrophe" into "the next great building site for the organization of mechanistic civilization."[13] We might say that Le Corbusier hoped to heal the wounds of Manhattan's modernity through a more intense modernism.

Although Le Corbusier's legacy for urban renewal and public housing is highly controversial today, his dreams for a vertical, post-Haussmann city do carry an explicit political component. Unlike his earlier vision, "La ville contemporaine" (1922), Radiant City ("La ville radieuse") makes a concerted effort to erase class segregation and focuses on planning as a means of "mobiliz[ing] property for human good."[14] Le Corbusier's integrated world of high-rise towers surrounded by large expanses of grass and open space, linked by aerial superhighways, aimed to address the chaos and collisions of the modern world, producing what Marshall Berman calls Le Corbusier's "modernized version of pastoral."[15] As Berman goes on to suggest, one of the central ironies of Le Corbusier's solutions to the physical/social/psychical turmoil of modern street life is in effect the erasure of street and people. Le Corbusier's dreams of a democratic cityscape ended up segregating people to compartments and monitored entrances with parking lots and underground garages as the only mediating and communal space.[16]

History tells us that these ideal cities—these giant machines—finally failed to address the classed, raced, and gendered realities embedded behind urban developments in America. And Le Corbusier himself has been justifiably criticized for his fascination with Harlem without understanding its socioeconomic conditions.[17] Yet the role of "Blackness" in Le Corbusier's thinking remains complex and offers a potential site of internal critique. In what follows, I want to venture to speculate that Le Corbusier's most democratizing ambitions are intimately bound up with his (often suppressed) sense of the impossibility of democratic architecture itself, an impossibility that arises precisely in those instances when he most *identifies* with the Black body.

To understand more fully Le Corbusier's relationship to radiant cities and dark bodies, let us turn to *Precisions: On the Present State of Architecture and City Planning*, an exuberant celebration of the ideas of the new modern building, body, human agency, and liberty. Like all high modernists, Le Corbusier saw himself as revolting against traditionalism. In proposing his famous *le plan libre* in contrast with what he called the "paralysis" of old masonry building, he argued that the modern house must be articulated and free like the human body, which is in turn like a machine, geared toward efficiency and economy.[18] We have already seen one vision of *le plan libre* in the drawing that I invoked earlier, which also came from *Precisions*, where Le Corbusier explicitly compared the modern house to the automobile and to the human body (figure 5.14).

But is the "free man" on which this "free plan" is based gender-neutral or just plain masculine? Where is this freedom and promise of new motility to come from? Let me suggest that one of the blueprints behind this modern, fully articulated, free modern man/city may be the figure of a racialized and "moving" woman: more specifically, the radiant, dark body of Baker.

Precisions represents a collection of lectures (interspersed with drawings improvised on blackboards, as well as journal-like notes) from Le Corbusier's lecture trip to Buenos Aires in the fall of 1929. It was also on this trip, six years prior to his New York visit, that Le Corbusier met Baker on the ocean liner *Giulio Cesare* on the way to Buenos Aires. Biographers of Baker and Le Corbusier alike agree that they enjoyed a romantic liaison during this period.[19] While in South America, they conducted separate tours but would reconvene occasionally. They then returned to Europe aboard the same ship, *Lutétia*. The impact of this relationship on his thinking about *le plan libre* would emerge in a sporadic but significant way throughout *Precisions*. In the section "A Dwelling on a Human Scale," Le Corbusier digresses into a personal reverie about life on board an ocean liner. He tells us that life on the ocean liner gives him a new sense of freedom in his own body:

> for fifteen days between Bordeaux and Buenos Aires, I am cut off from the rest of the world. . . . I open my trunks, I settle in my house, I'm in the skin of a gentleman who has rented a small house.[20]

That Le Corbusier should find escapism on board a ship, adrift between national boundaries and temporarily free from bourgeois habits, is not surprising, but that that freedom should express itself as a series of borrowed bodily containers is much more disconcerting.

Ensconced within the steel body of the ocean liner, suspended in what Freud would call the undifferentiated state of the "oceanic," Le Corbusier discovers "the rest of the world"—not through adventure or motion but through stillness and serial confinement: a trunk, a body as housing, a housing that turns out to be a rental. This dream of subjective fulfillment is also a dream of depersonalization. Much of the European primitivist discourse has been boiled down as a formula about escapism, self-reinvigoration, and self-making at the expense of the racial other. And Le Corbusier's musings here easily fit into that classic narrative. Yet why does the escapism here sound like imprisonment, and self-discovery like self-*un*making? Why is the comfort of habitation also so tomblike? Is it because the specter of the Middle Passage, a horrific version of oceanic suspension, haunts this passage and ties the dream of freedom eerily close to dreams of profound constraint?

Not coincidentally, this is also where Le Corbusier first mentions Baker:

To rise above oneself is a profoundly individual act. One doesn't do so with second-hand clothing . . . but with this which is nothing but is everything: with proportions. Proportions are a series of interacting relationships. . . .

When Josephine Baker on November 27, 1919, in Sao Paulo, in an idiotic music hall show, sings, "Baby," she brings to it such an intense and dramatic sensitivity that tears rush to my eyes.

In her steamship cabin, she picks up a little guitar—a child's toy— that someone gave her and sings all the black songs: ". . . you're the weave of the cloth and I put all you are in the cloth, I roll it up and take it away. . . ."

She lives all over the world. She moves immense crowds. So there is a real heart in crowds? . . . Man . . . has to be torn away from the abominable lies that make a hell of his life.[21]

This account is discombobulating in more ways than one. Is the first paragraph about the transcendent artist a reference to himself, or to Baker, or both? Who is the subject or the object of those lines? Why the metaphor of "second-hand clothing"? What does that (or, come to think of it, its alternative) signify? Art, it would appear, cannot be born from secondhand clothing. But we know from the section entitled "A Dwelling on a Human Scale," quoted earlier, that being in someone's borrowed skin can be comforting. In fact, is not Le Corbusier himself just such "second-hand clothing" in that other passage? Does this mean that "good" borrowings are those that enact originariness or can somehow be ontologically revising? And why should we be getting an inversion of the emperor's clothes, where the male mind longs for rags, for perforated skins whose "containing function"[22] is at risk?

What interests me about Le Corbusier's account of primitivist euphoria is its obsession with the possibilities of what might be called onto-sartorial exchanges in "a series of interacting relationships." The seduction that Baker represents in this account is less the call of the siren than the call of the mother ("Baby"). In the steamship cabin, that makeshift nursery, holding a "child's" guitar, Baker's voice brings Le Corbusier to tears. In this maternal, artistic, and ecstatic moment, being "moved" is to be moved outside of oneself, a dream of pleasurable disembodiment and demasculinization. And Baker herself also seems more a medium than an authentic source: she sings "the black songs" as if they were a repertoire that she borrows; she does not quite fit the space (that "idiotic music hall"); her instrument is not quite her own. Thus, what transforms Le Corbusier's bourgeois complacency into transcendence—what allows him to break out of his own skin, so to speak—is, first, the dynamic and moving cover of Baker covering Black music and, second, the *gift* of recognizing the essential borrowedness of his own skin. If this is racial appropriation, it is a very curious and mediated form of taking. Instead of self-possession, we are seeing a yearning for evaporation.

And the nature of this particular "Black mother" is odd, too. If history tells us that the Black mammy has been succoring white men for a long time and if psychoanalysis tells us that the maternal voice provides a "sonorous envelope" (with both comforting and suffocating potentials), then this scene of Black maternal call does *not* quite fit either script.[23] It is noticeable that Le Corbusier, who started out his career as a painter, locates Baker's power not in her appearance but in her voice. The quality of Baker's voice is controversial and was a source of constant vexation for Baker herself, who repeatedly took voice lessons to improve it. Some who first knew her by name and sight were thrilled by her appearance but disappointed by her voice, which has been alternately labeled by critics as thin, reedy, squeaky, shrill, and twittering.[24] This (often American) public dissatisfaction, even critical meanness, about Baker's voice reveals some things about the nature of her iconography, the history of expectation surrounding the American Black female voice, and, finally, Le Corbusier's investment in it.

Just as critics have taken Baker's performance style as a given, little or no attention has been paid to the strangely and impressively mercurial quality and range of her voice. One might readily identify a Baker song (for example, "J'ai deux amours") but not the Baker voice. The myth is that she did not have much of a voice, but the range of her voice is in fact remarkable. The timbre of her voice travels from the high-pitched, shrill upper tones of something like her film singing in *Princesse Tam Tam*, to the medium, choppy, ornery brightness of "Don't Touch My Tomatoes," to the smooth, warm bottom tones of "Sonny Boy."[25] This acrobatic range says something about the diverse genres and traditions in which she performed (from the musical stage and its vaudeville roots to films to studio recording to even the opera), but it also tells us something about her skills.[26] It explains, too, why American audiences in particular were not receptive to Baker's voice. For if the female voice, like telltale tears, is supposed to be an authentic and audible sign of interiority, Baker's "queer" voice clearly did not participate fully or traditionally in the much more venerated tradition of the diva blues—and the assumption of Black female embodiment that that genre presumes.

So which Baker voice did Le Corbusier hear on board that steamship? We, of course, cannot say for certain. What we do know is that the "mother" Le Corbusier found in her was not exactly the succoring Black mother, for his descriptions of that voice suggest a sonic quality that penetrates rather than embraces, jars rather than soothes. Could it be that the Baker voice that moves Le Corbusier to tears in the confines of that cabin is the Baker voice of the sharp register, the voice of Zouzou the caged bird?

In the film *Zouzou* (directed by Marc Allégret, 1934; figure 6.1), Baker, swinging inside a life-size gilded birdcage, gives a tingling rendition of the song "Haiti" in a high, tinny, hollowed-out voice (even at moments twittering) that wavers somewhere between the cries of a small bird and a recorder, turning the sonic into the semiotic, tuning to perfection the twinning of animation and mechanization, of artistic expression and the grounding conditions of its flight. Indeed, the tension between liberty and confinement, so pressing in Le Corbusier's passage on Baker and echoing the same tension that suffuses much of Le Corbusier's self-descriptions in *Precisions*, suggests to us that what draws Le Corbusier to Baker's voice may in fact be not its warmth but its sharpness. Indeed, according to him, Baker's voice would seem to have a *thinning* quality. For the garment of maternal envelope that Le Corbusier imagines Baker to be providing is not only not fantasized as thick or warm but downright cutting. This mother turns out to be a rather ruthless seamstress: one who cuts, peels, and reproportions her child. This maternal tailor (even architect) bares her subject, then refabricates his interiority into pure surface ("you're the weave of the cloth and I put all you are in the cloth"), and then discards it/him ("I roll it up and take it away"). This mother dresses and flays in the same gesture.

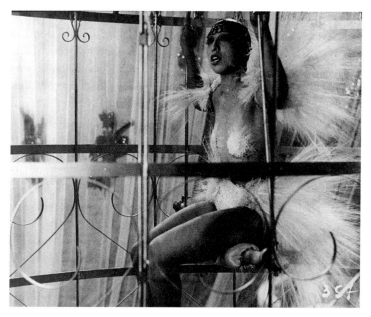

Fig. 6.1
Freedom and need are not opposed, but rather, conditions of one another.
—*Wendy Brown*

The Baker of Le Corbusier's fantasy turns out to be an agent who recuts his skin and reproportions his very being. We may now have a different and potentially deeper sense of how we understand this man, famous for his white walls and who once wrote to a client that "[we] have got used to compositions which are so complicated that they give the impression often of men carrying their intestines outside of their bodies. . . . We claim that these should remain inside . . . and that the outside of the house should appear in all its limpidity."[27] Filtered through Le Corbusier's meditations on Baker, we begin to suspect that the limpid (masculine, impassive) surface may not be oppositional to (feminized) raw nerves but precisely their stripped expression. Just as Baker's voice reveals the problematic accord, rather than separation, between essence and performance, Le Corbusier's famous limpid façade invokes, rather than dispels, the contagious contact between surface and interiority. His dream of a cloaking freedom is at once inspired and pierced by Baker, a figure of haunting alienation.

One night, on their way back to Europe, Le Corbusier shows up at a ball on board the *Lutétia* dressed as Baker, with darkened skin and feathers glued to his body.[28] Given their personal intimacy, her actual presence at the event, and, not least of all, the confession above, what do we make of this makeover? In addition to the obvious possibilities of parody or tribute, we are compelled to intuit also the psychical and affective forces mobilizing this act of cross-racial and cross-gender masquerade. What makes this scene more than what it initially appears (a case of ill-judged homage) is the profound exposure of Le Corbusier himself. If Baker has played the orphan many times (from "Chocolate Dandies" to *Zouzou* to *Princesse Tam Tam*), it is Le Corbusier who now steals the role. For it is not Baker's reputed Americanness or Africanness that Le Corbusier potentially mimes but her transcendental homelessness. The cosmopolitan subject ("She lives all over the world") is, of course, also a homeless and stateless subject. The Baker who moves Le Corbusier is the Baker who is out of place. There is an intense longing here on Le Corbusier's part during this voyage to be released from the burdens of social and identificatory confinements, to be orphaned and radically at sea, so to speak, and it is perhaps at *this* level that Le Corbusier and Baker, these two very public subjects living in very different contexts and possessing very different powers and limitations, found their affinity.

The ideal conceptualization of a "dwelling at a human scale" is melancholically born out of a state of exception: both Le Corbusier's own imagined hiatus from nation and class (the "abominable lies" that trap man) *and* his entangled dreams of being stripped and taken by a dark woman whose liberty in the world has been purchased at the price of forever being seen as performing the signs of inhumanity and unfreedom.

When Baker sees Le Corbusier at the ball, she exclaims, "What a pity you are an architect, Monsieur. You'd make a sensational partner."[29] (How else to deal with your lover coming to dinner dressed *as* your theater costume?) This response is so soigné that one is reminded of the kinds of verbal skins that Baker must have developed throughout her career. Yet it is precisely the question of skin—what it can or fails to reveal, protect, or own—that connects Baker to her admirers in ways that say much about the nature of modernism and its dreams of subjecthood and objecthood. In the story of Baker and Le Corbusier, we witness a series of mutual projections: she turns him inside out and weaves fabric out of him; he turns himself into the pure surface of her voice. She makes a diva out of him; he makes an architect out of her.

If architecture can be seen as an ally in inhabitation, then it also points us to the profound challenges inhering in the acts of inhabiting and connecting ourselves, both to places and to our own bodies. The dream of the skyscraper is another dream of a second skin, one that also reveals the profound and perhaps finally utopic desire to refabricate human geography as bodies, places, and nations. Le Corbusier's contact with Baker did not enable him to build the Radiant City; instead, it unraveled his manifestos of freedom and home. The vision of a Radiant City (of an architecture whose pristine brightness then can accommodate the heterogeneity of modern life) is haunted by the remembrance of alternative spaces. Le Corbusier's plans for the Radiant City were never fulfilled except as diffused and corrupted concepts that ended up exacerbating the very urban plights it was meant to assuage. Perhaps modernists such as Loos and Le Corbusier came to Baker (and stayed and stayed, to borrow Picasso's formulation) because they saw in her the self-same philosophical and aesthetic crisis about subjectivity caught between ideals of public impersonality and embodied privacy.

The point here is not that European modernity is built on the suppression of the nostalgia for the atavism that it reviles but that the complications engendered by this disavowal repeatedly avow themselves and are embodied within the very figuration of the modern object. From Baker's banana skirt to her golden cladding to Loos's Baker House to Le Corbusier's white cities, we are looking not at hidden depths or longings but at the material traces of a desire that is written on the skin/surface again and again, like striated lines. In the end, could it be that it is the experience of another kind of freedom—one that is not marked and perhaps not even free at all—that can only be found at sea that drives Le Corbusier to dress as Baker, to borrow her skin? In those moments when Le Corbusier dresses himself as Baker, are we seeing the pleasures of an exquisite, transitory dwelling? Moreover, could it be that this thieving paradoxically enables the possibility of an identification not available otherwise? For it is often the case that it is through the occupation of an impossible place, through the usurpation of a place not proper to ourselves, that we gain the most intense and sympathetic insights into that which does not contain us.

And can we now return to "the depths on the ninetieth floor" and see in the shadow of the pailletted woman the silhouette of the songwriter himself, the gay man who wrote the most beautiful love songs in the world?

7

The Woman with the Golden Skin

Charlotte Perriand (1903–1999), the French architect and designer who worked with Le Corbusier and became known at age twenty-four for "Bar under the Roof," a line of furniture made out of chromed steel and anodized aluminum, once identified herself with Baker precisely as an embodiment of steely modernity:

> I am conscious of and in synch with my times. They are mechanical: in the streets the beautiful cars wink at me, they are clean, shining. I adorn my neck with chromed-steel beads, my waist with a coat of mail, my studio with chromed steel. I wear my hair à la Josephine Baker.[1]

We are, in short, looking at another pailletted woman. Perriand's sleek vision of modernism clads itself in primitive armors (neck beads, coat of mail), instantiating the simultaneity of pastness and futurity. However, instead of seeing Josephine Baker as the object onto which the inherent contradiction of modernism has been projected, let us attend to the ways in which Baker's sartorial nakedness invokes and draws energy from the frisson between *flesh* and *objectness* underlying modernism's fascination with surface.

To get at this interplay between flesh and materialness, let us turn to Baker's famous "sculpturalness," a quality much noted by both men and women. Janet Flanner called her an "unforgettable female ebony statue"; André Levinson pronounced her to be the "finest example of Negro sculpture"; Hanry-Jaunet proclaimed her body to be "always sculptural."[2] This attribution has mostly been taken to reference European primitivism's long-standing engagement with tribal art and objects, especially African sculptures, which were celebrated by modernists such as Alberto Giacometti not for their "fleshly" quality but for their presumed formal abstractions. In *Primitivism in 20th*

Second Skin. Second edition. Anne Anlin Cheng, Oxford University Press. © Oxford University Press 2023.
DOI: 10.1093/oso/9780197748381.003.0007

Century Art: Affinity of the Tribal and the Modern, William Rubin argues that while African and Oceanic tribal objects have been in circulation in Europe since the mid-nineteenth century, it took the modernists to revise the aesthetic terms on which those objects have been understood.[3] Artists like Pablo Picasso and Georges Braque, Rubin suggests, exhibit an artistic empathy for an altogether different kind of tribal object from what was previously favored. In Picasso's case, for instance, instead of "classically" ethnographic objects associated with realism, brute matter, and sensuality, he prefers those that are abstract, formal (nonanecdotal), even "unfinished."[4] It is the *conceptual* quality in the African sculptures and objects in question that launches the modernist move away from "narrative images" to more frontal and "iconic" ones.[5] In short, for Rubin, we are looking at the early beginnings of what we now consider conceptual art.

The quality of abstraction thus has always accompanied the discourse of primitive organicity. At the same time, however, there remains in Rubin's work a sense that conceptualization as an intellectual and imaginative activity resides solely on the part of the Western modern artist doing the looking and that the inert "primitive" object can be rediscovered, fractured or otherwise, as recognizable, material elements in modern art. So Rubin can trace one component of a Picasso painting to, say, an Iberian rather than an African mask. Even Rosalind Krauss's elegant and well-known critique of Rubin and of the memorable "Primitivism" exhibition at the Museum of Modern Art unwittingly reproduces the distinction between Western thought and "primitive objects." As many recall, Krauss makes the important intervention against Rubin's influence-study model by arguing that we must see "primitive objects" as not "historical" but "theoretical objects"; the latter she defines as "an analysis of the way that Western, formalist culture constructs meaning" and as "a powerful shaping tool, a way of rethinking all fields within the human sciences."[6] Her formulation, however, does not quite rescue those objects from what she calls their "neutralized" state in modernist primitivist discourse. What remains unquestioned is the boundary separating Western subjectivity and primitive objectness, between Western intellectuality and non-Western things; in her words, "[T]he value of the primitive was, quite simply, what it enabled *one to think*."[7] There is little question who the "one" is doing the thinking here. The "primitive object" remains neutralized and inert: a screen, a tool.

We, on the other hand, have been tracing the intricate ways in which modernist artists and projects are themselves profoundly transformed through the process of engaging with the imagined racial other/object. Adolf Loos's Baker House, for instance, even if intended as an architectural incorporation of the corporeal Baker, ends up becoming a site for an involved, conceptual engagement with the very notion of abstraction in her theatrical art, a confrontation that pushes back on the pressure points in his own theoretical work, as well as highlighting the intricacies and contradictions inhering in racial and sexual identities. Moreover, the so-called objects, even in their most isolated and reified states, can not only affect how they are looked at but also revise the modality of display aimed to capture them.

Even in real life, Baker herself enjoyed a complicated relationship with the category of "tribal objects." As Bennetta Jules-Rosette tells us, in the early decades of the twentieth century in France, museums and show business shared an economic, not just ideological, partnership.[8] In 1925, the year Baker arrived in Paris, three young anthropologists, Marcel Mauss, Lucien Lévy-Bruhl, and Paul Rivet, established the Institut d'Ethnologie with a specific plan to reorganize the Musée de Trocadéro, where Picasso had his vertiginous encounter some eighteen years before. They enlisted the help of Georges-Henri Rivière, who adored Baker and the music hall and who introduced wax dioramas resembling music-hall tableaux to the museum. According to the biographer, Baker helped Rivière raise funds for the 1931 Dakar-Djibouti anthropological expedition, a trans-African mission that would collect and document artifacts and languages. And so when Jules-Rosette asserts that by the time the new Musée de l'Homme (where the infamous display of Saartjie Baartman/Venus Hottentot's dissected genitals would be on view for decades to come) opened in 1931, Baker had "begun to marshal the emblems of her performative primitivism to the aid of avid collectors,"[9] we have to ask, who is the source of the "taste" being disciplined here? Who is training whom? Who is the collector and who the collected? This convoluted history of exchange, commodification, agency, and collection documented by Jules-Rosette deeply complicates how we understand what constitutes originary source versus appropriation and the epistemological mastery that they connote when it comes to the mobile relationship between "modern art" and "primitive object."

When it comes to Baker's art and iconography, the question of objectness and objecthood remains just as intricate, for her image draws on fantasies of both abstraction and materiality in ways that confound those terms, as well as reorganize how those terms relate to racial and sexual differences. In what follows, I want to take a close look at Baker's presence in photography. While nineteenth-century ethnography, modern theatrical entertainment, and the museum share visual and ideological vocabularies when it comes to staging the racialized body, this insight should not blind us to the difference in the ways in which Black skin begins to be represented in celluloid at the dawn of the twentieth century. What E. E. Cummings observed about Baker (that she was "neither infrahuman nor superhuman") signals primitivist fantasy and exaggeration, but it also pinpoints a peculiar quality about Baker as an aesthetic object, one that captures her strangely fluid relation to the organic and the inorganic. As we have already begun to see via Baker's film work, when it comes to Baker-the-visual-icon, skin does not equal flesh—a decoupling that will, as we are about to see, unsettle some very basic assumptions about racialized skin.

Baker's odd relationship to both others' skins and her own skin has been, I would argue, most dramatically distilled in the archive of her studio photographs. This archive (see figures 7.1–7.4) includes some of the most enduring and mesmerizing photographs of Baker, taken by well-known photographers such as the Viennese photographer Dora Kalmuss, alias Madame d'Ora, and the French photographer George Hoyningen-Huene.

These images arrest the eye for several reasons. They embody the highly wrought glamour traditions of Hollywood, associated with photographers such as Ruth Harriet Louise and George Hurrell. To say this, however, is to raise a set of absorbing questions about Baker, photography, celebrity, and skin. This is indeed the first time that Black skin is, and can be, glamorized. But the point here is not just that Baker assumes a look that has traditionally and ideologically been reserved for white femininity—an amazing and notable fact in itself—but also,

Fig. 7.1

Fig. 7.2

Fig. 7.3

Fig. 7.4

and more important, they raise a nexus of intriguing questions about the surfacism of Black skin at the turn of the twentieth century.

These nude images rely, oxymoronically, on the composition of layered surfaces. Baker's skin is constantly referring to other surfaces and textuals. Her seminudity is invariably accompanied by three visual tropes that have become her visual signatures: animal fur, that almost ubiquitous gold cloth, and dark shadows. We can dismiss these ornamental details as the clichéd conflation between animalism and dark, racialized female sexuality. But by now we are sensitive to the complications of skin and surface in Baker's art. Does human skin (both literal and displaced by the aforementioned tropes) in these images act as decoration or cladding? Is "Blackness" ornament or essence? And what would it mean for "ornament" to acquire or require "essence" and vice versa?

To ask these questions is already to acknowledge skin's potential for surrogacy. The onlooker, for instance, might begin to observe how the lighting and the mise-en-scène work to conflate the different registers of surface planes. Thus, Baker's Black, airbrushed, and seemingly flawless skin—greased and polished to a shiny, laminated gloss—finds an echo in her sleek, metallicized hair that, in turn, recovers itself in the lamé cloth pouring out of her body. In these images, the spill and shimmer of light across the surface minimalize the three-dimensional materiality of the body. Indeed, light becomes a kind of prosthetic skin for Baker, rendering the idea of skin itself as costume, prop, and surrogate. The masculinist/impassive/technological modern surfaces (bronze, metal, shellac, film) flow casually into the feminized/animalized/fluid surfaces (skin, cloth, hair) in these images. What is so sexy about these images is not so much Baker's naked body as its surfaceness and that quality's ability to express and facilitate fluidity.

Baker's glamour shots thus compel us to reconsider the relationship between skin and what cultural theorist Richard Dyer calls Hollywood's "cult of light." For Dyer, this cult of light is part of a much larger romance with race, colonialism, and Christianity. In *White*, he famously argues that classic Hollywood lighting, reflecting the centrality of whiteness in Western visual culture which is in turn dependent on the concomitant ideals of Christian and white-racial purity, is made for white women and for *whitening* women.[10] (He speaks, for instance, of the cinematic fetishization of the "white face" and Hollywood's persistent use of carbon arc lamps instead of incandescent tungsten light, even thought the latter was much less expensive and much easier to handle because it tended to bring out colors in all subjects, including white faces.) Black actresses from Dorothy Dandridge to Lena Horne have stories to tell of how standard Hollywood lighting has not been kind to them.

But Baker proves to be the exception that is instructive: far from wilting under its force, she appears to reflect or even absorb telescopic light itself. From her famous lacquered hair, known as the "Baker Do," to the expanse of gleaming skin in her studio photographs, Baker sheen is an integral part of her iconography. (In these images as well as other studio photographs, Baker's skin is often, if not always, anointed by oils that in turn enhance, even mime, the lighting that falls on it.) The questions are: Is this an animalistic shine, to which Dyer reminds us that Hollywood photographers of female stars are highly allergic since shine connotes sweat and an unwelcomed instance of the body's dirt?[11] Or is it an inorganic luster, a laminated quality that gestures to an alternative tradition of diva photography? And, ultimately, is glamour's lamination always and never more than commodity fetishism?

To answer these questions, we have to reconsider the quality of light in these images in relation to three distinct but entwined contexts: the history of Hollywood lighting, industrial and hence material revolution, and sculptural discourses in the interwar period. Baker's hard sheen suggests that even within the mainstream world of Hollywood lighting for white female stars, there was at least one other mode of lighting than the one identified by Dyer: one that is exemplified by the glossy lure of Marion Davies, Gloria Swanson, Marlene Dietrich, Joan Crawford, Greta Garbo, and Jean Harlow, for whom the romance of shellacked beauty wields the pull of endless fascination.

This lighting distinguishes itself from the soft, pearlized surface underscored by Dyer and applied to women such as Lillian Gish or, later, Marilyn Monroe. In the cases of Gish and Monroe, the lighting emphasizes the women's childlike femininity, their vulnerable tenderness and availability. The almost electroplated lighting that we are seeing with Harlow and Baker is qualitatively different: its tonality and texture harder, more synthetic, more properly a *finish*. We are beholding a promise of erotic materiality that is self-consciously inorganic. (As Roland Barthes observed, someone like Garbo impresses on the observer the force of a beauty that is inhumanly flawless, preserved in perfection.)[12] Similarly, Baker sheen does not recall the labor of human sweat but exudes instead the cool sheen of metals, rendering these images at once hot and cool.

To be sure, we can readily read this glamorous perfection as but another instance of female objectification. Within this understanding, figures like Harlow (figure 7.5) would provide clear examples of how

Fig. 7.5
An ideally shaped machine.... At one end, raw, telluric matter, at the other, the finished, human object.
—*Roland Barthes*

white female epidermal surfaces (from flawless skin to a perfectly shaped glass tear on the cheek to the celluloid sheen of hair) were uniformly transformed in the early twentieth century into synthetic surfaces for fan consumption. And the Black female skin, with its extensive history of objectification, commodification, and abuse, when made visible through a similar visual rhetoric, simply offers an even more intense story about the reification and consumption of female skin. This account, while accurate, nonetheless misses something about the fantasies that in the early century were invested into the *life* and *seduction* of synthetic surfaces. For in addition to the abject history of the objectification of the racialized female body, we have to bring to bear on Baker's image a sense of what Judith Brown calls the "early-century semiotics of plastics."[13] The invention of plastic, that most twentieth-century of materials, Brown contends, ushered in an age of technological euphoria that spoke the language and imagination of synthetic chemistry. Industrial designers, artists, photographers, and even writers (here Brown urges that we think of Gertrude Stein and Ezra Pound) shared mercurial dreams of a flat, clean, denuded, endlessly appealing glossy surface. As Jeffrey L. Meikle points out, the new materials of the early twentieth century (fabricated plastics from celluloid to Bakelite to nylon that can be "molded, extruded, foamed, stamped, vacuum-formed") engendered not only new industrial inventions and new consumer appetites but also a larger cultural desire for and faith in the possibilities of infinite transformations.[14] This sense of a dynamically moldable plasticity—of a body that can follow as well as lead molten gold—infuses photographic representations of Baker.

Baker's incandescent, sculptural figure also urges us to turn to another "cult of light": the discourse of "shine" and sculptural surfaces in the 1920s and 1930s. As art historian Jon Wood suggests, artists in that period were enthralled by shine, which symbolized for artists such as Constantin Brancusi and Henry Moore a host of ideas, including most notably ideas about auratic potential and originary radiance.[15] Through shine itself, artists believed they could release sculpture from its material condition and open it up to new meanings. In discussing how sculptors deploy shine to "enhance curve" and "lead the eye around," Wood points us toward the possibility that shine has become more than a description or a quality of light but the very *medium*

through which the visual and the sensorial merge. In short, I am interested in shine *as* relationality. Hence Baker lacquer, instead of repeating a rhetoric of corporeal residue (i.e., sweat), functions to release
or open up the body from its corporeal limits by linking it to metallur-
gical, plastic, and other synthetic materials. And fabrics like silk and
fur in turn aim to simulate skin and render a kind of tangible and emo-
tional hypersensitivity.[16] Thus, with an image like the vertical, frontal
shot of Baker by Hoyningen-Huene (figure 7.1), we can suddenly see a
reworking of Elie Nadelman's "Man in Open Air." Instead of the highly
organic (and degrading) shine long associated with Black skin since
the sixteenth century, Baker skin, refracted through the new discourse
of auratic plasticity, underscores the mutual longings and fantasies of
impenetrable skin.[17] It is not just that "bare life," as Giorgio Agamben
would say, can be turned into a thing but also that thingness might
embody agency or life.[18] The dream of the sensible *and* the dream of
the insensible appear seductively identical. Sheen, as that which both
attracts and repels vision, plays hide-and-seek with visual satisfaction
and produces a sexy interplay between the scopic and the haptic: are
we looking, or are we feeling?

We might say that these photos give us not skin but skin sense. The
effect I am trying to locate here is related to what Bill Brown calls the
"indeterminate ontology" of modern objects, the inability to fully separate the animate from the inanimate.[19] In photography, a medium
that bears an inherently ambivalent relationship to life and inanimacy,
presence and absence, we find Baker's most stunning and intriguing
engagement with the visual limits of what constitutes the human, the
animal, and the manufactured. Baker appears in these photographs as
sculptural rather than visceral, cut rather than voluptuous. Her polished and flawless skin suggests bronze rather than flesh; the splendid
silk and the glimmer of thigh echo each other. Her figure, often firmly
outlined with dark lines, appears almost embossed on the photographic paper, sharing its glossy textuality—in short, producing an os-
cillation between portrait and still life.

We can read this "ontological democratization," to borrow once
again from Bill Brown,[20] as another instance of the objectification
of Baker, and my task here is not to deny or absolve that fact but to
point out how that very process of objectification—even as it takes

subjectivity from her—*also* invests the objects around her with sub-jectivity, which in turn provides a kind of cloak for her nakedness. In short, objectification can be a kind of covering, too. Baker iconography itself constantly invokes the slippage between skin and cloth, the real and the conceptual. What makes Baker so affectively magnetic and in-tellectually stirring for modernists may not be her sculptural quality in that trial-art-object sense but precisely her mobile and vibrant play with "skin" as cladding: a covering at once itinerant (transferable) and inchoative (in the process of *becoming*).

If today we are less receptive to the expression of the potentiality between aesthetic style and ontological presence, between thingness and agency, it is partially because we no longer share the ideal of plas-ticity or shine rooted in early-century *material nova*. If materials like plastics, Bakelite, and celluloid promised a new compatibility between the organic and the inorganic, then by the mid-twentieth century, the larger generic category of plastics had degraded to associations with things cheap, insipid, and painfully artificial.[21] Similarly, the matte has replaced sheen as a sign of taste. These shifts from attachment to repul-sion for shine and plastics have much to do with our current culture's truncated capacity to experience glamour (itself a surface lure) in quite the same way. Glamour today is essentially a nostalgic category no matter how some might protest otherwise. It has faded from our lives, not because all the great movie stars and divas have vanished but be-cause the rich blankness of synthetic lives ushered in by early-century technological inventions and the crisis of personhood that these new inventions and materials in turn engendered have become less jarring, less urgent, less promising. The beckoning emptiness of the modern age, what Thomas Hardy called "the ache of modernism,"[22] has slipped into normative loss and daily emptiness. Indeed, we have come to see the virtue of a life without aura: we call it democracy. (This is why fashion today means replication, why contemporary celebrity culture is more about the advertisement of emulation than the privilege of in-imitability. This is why we renounce royalty only to canonize "Princess Di," who had the dubiously enviable ability to have domestic problems like everyone else. What appears to be an ideological oxymoron in American society today—a stout-hearted democracy that boasts of an unbridled celebrity culture—is really the fundamental paradox

founding the birth of the modern cult of celebrity: the celebration of the inimitable individual who promises the possibilities of replication, the everyday, and emulation.)

Baker's early-century studio photographs thus provide crucial archival evidence of a pivotal moment in which the tradition of the nineteenth-century painted portrait is about to turn into but not yet become contemporary paparazzi images. The grand genre of portraiture and contemporary publicity images bookend on both sides a history and range of subject representations, from a cult of presumably exceptional personality to its all-too-reproducible commodification. If the Victorian portrait was all about unique possession and unique individuals and contemporary celebrity culture all about mass replication and thing-as-commodity (that is, we have replaced the portrait with the primacy of commodity), then Baker's so-called studio art photography sits somewhere in between.[23]

Baker in these images registers (rather than veils or overlooks) the taut intimacy between *thingness* and *personality*. These images present a somewhat hybrid genre that both turns persons and things into commodities and yet works to animate them. How do the effects of Baker's objectness impact our own sense of subjectivity? Does it make claims on our ontology as viewers? What happens to our own sense of subjectivity when we look at a portrait that reminds us of the confusion between the artificial and the organic, between life and death? These are all ways of also asking why we enjoy looking at a still life, at, say, a bowl of fruit. Mark Seltzer would tell us very wisely that the still life provides an artificial synecdoche for life, for consumption itself.[24] But could it also be the case that we like looking at still life because *it allows us to be still*?

Could it be that the woman-as-fruit is pleasurable both because she/it can be consumed *and* because she/it cannot be eaten, a strange fruit? (Is this not one of the reasons we like to look at a Vermeer? The comforting stillness of the human figure always slipping into the beautiful stillness of light and silence of table, and the promise of the human becoming most keen when it rests within and disappears into the sheen of one teary pearl earring?) So, commodified, yes, but also strangely unconsumable. Seeing the Baker images as a new kind of *vanitas* helps us reconsider the relationship between enduring objectness and racialized/feminized flesh. I am trying to suggest, counterintuitively, that it may be the plasticity and metallurgy of Baker imagery that render it most resistant to consumption. That is, given that the most politically troubling aspect of Baker's visual legacy has been its presumed acquiescence to the objectification of the racialized, female body, we may consider how Baker's ability to escape into surfaces paradoxically allows her image to deflect misogynist and racist logic. It may even offer an important critique of (or at least an alternative response to) the discourse of flesh designed to rescue that captive body from that history of objectification.

Feminists and race critics have been invested in recovering the flesh made into "thing" and then devastated. That is, if the captive Black female body has provided a rich source of irresistible and destructive sensuality, turning that body into a "thing" ("being for the captor"), then "flesh" with all its material fissures, tears, scars, and ruptures serves as a crucial and ethical reminder of the injuries inflicted on that body.[25] I am alluding liberally to the work of Hortense Spillers here because it offers one of the most important and cogent feminist interventions into the discourse of the body as it intersects with the history of the Black female body. For Spillers, this violent writing on the body reads like a tattoo:

> These undecipherable markings on the captive body render a kind of hieroglyphics of the flesh whose severe disjunctions come to be hidden to the cultural seeing by skin color.[26]

But I am signaling here the ways in which Baker, especially in these images, suggests and enacts a different kind of body thing and body writing. Her molten skin appears impervious not only to the kind of primitive tattoo detailed by Loos but also to the kind of marking identified by Spillers. This is, of course, not to say that Baker as a person and performer has not suffered racial markings but to recognize that her nakedness in performance might be refuting or even doing the work of suturing those ruptures. Moreover, it is a "healing" that draws *not* from some essentialized notion of prediscursive flesh or recuperated embodiment but from the vocabulary/cladding of the plastic sense that I have described. It is the plastic sense lent to her figuration that turns her from a body suffering from or disguising the "hieroglyphics of the flesh" into a figure that stands resistant to them. What renders these images not quite "pornotropes"[27] is their *sealedness*.

Consequently, the distinction between the nude and the naked, as the classic distinction between higher and lower forms of visual pleasures (and objects), blurs—not because one is but a euphemism for the other but because the "artistic" and the "pornographic" are shown to be preconditions for each other. In these images, flesh reveals itself as style, even as style becomes discernible only through its simulation of the corporeal. Baker appears at once wholly available and wholly into herself. In light of the persistent fantasy of possession that characterizes masculinist imperial imagination, the emptying out of subjectivity on the part of the object can actually and perversely feel like a relief to us. (Could this be why shadows play such a bodily presence in these images, often looming larger than the subject herself? *Being for the other* has turned into *being for the self*?)[28]

The politics of embodiment and subjectivity for a woman of color has always been a tricky business. Our culture is quick to assign personhood and agency to those long deprived of both, but this gift is often granted at the expense of recognizing or even allowing those inevitable moments when the exceptionalism of subjectivity fails. By the exceptionalism of subjectivity, I am referring to received concepts of individualism, assumed by traditions such as American exceptionalism that implicitly presume and privilege an ideal of a subject who is integrated, authentic, or whole. The premium we place on subjectivity as an antidote against discrimination and other forms of social objectification is understandable, but, as I am trying to suggest here, subjectivity gets invoked too often precisely at those very moments when its condition for being is most at risk.

This, then, is Baker's response to the injunction of injured subjectivity. This is *her* dream of a second skin, a desire that is shared both by modernists seeking to be outside their own skins and by racialized subjects looking to free themselves from the burden of racial legibility. I have been trying to trace an agency at work in these images—by locating it not in Baker's intentions but literally on the surface, on its very fibers. If the portrait offers the promise of a person and the still life the promise of a thing, then the Baker photography that we are examining here brings us not fulfillment but the (specifically photographic) pleasure of suspension: that pause or delay before a person becomes a person and a thing a thing. To lose oneself in these images is to surrender to a drama about the immanent possibilities of personhood and its frightening-yet-seductive affinity for objectness.

Let us now turn to a term whose specter haunts this discussion about objectness: the machine. The connection between femininity and machinery has been around since the writings of Frederick Winslow Taylor and the methods of Henry Ford both swept Europe before World War I with their promises of more efficient modes of production and the scientific management of the human body. Seltzer suggests that America's turn-of-the-century fascination with technology inheres not simply in the notions that machines can replace bodies and persons, or that persons are already machines, or even that technologies make bodies, but in the "radical and intimate *coupling* of bodies and machines."[29] He also demonstrates how masculinity at the turn of the century was disciplined and narrativized through Taylorism. But, as Martha Banta and Jennifer L. Fleissner point out, the female body does not escape this dream of pristine management. There grew an increasing association between femininity and machinery as a means of deploying, disciplining, and controlling anxieties about "wayward" female bodies. Taylorism narrates and structures the female body in factories, offices, and kitchens and onstage. In the realm of entertainment, we get the phenomenon of precision dancing and chorus-girl troupes such as the Tiller Girls, the Ziegfeld Girls, the Alfred Jackson Girls, and the Busby Berkeley Girls. In fact, in his 1931 essay "Girls and Crisis," Siegfried Kracauer would come to describe these female dance troupes as a precision apparatus: what he calls "a machine of girls," epitomizing the optimism of American capitalism and mechanical success.[30]

Addressing the dysphoria underlying these dreams of female efficiency and management, Fleissner reminds us that it is mostly on the female body that Taylorism reveals its keen predilection for compulsion. Fleissner's terminology resonates against Baker's dancing body because the latter both instantiates and recasts the idea of compulsion.

Consider the following descriptions of Baker and how they conflate kinesthetics, animality, femininity, and technology:

> She enters through a dense electric twilight.
> —E. E. Cummings

> [Her] flawless torso and whirl-wind limbs . . . speeding and stamping . . . free, perfect, and exact . . . round the dynamic hips.
> —Nancy Cunard

> [Her] bold dislocations, her springing movements.
> —André Levinson

> performing a series of movements without ever losing the basic pattern. . . . She never even gets hot, her skin remains fresh, cool, dry . . . one of George Grosz's mechanical dolls.
> —Count Kessler

> This is not a woman, not a dancer . . . you might call it ectoplasm.
> —Rene Régnier

Baker's dancing is remembered less for its choreographic precision than for its overwhelming energy, its almost frenetic motion. Dance scholar Andre Lepecki has argued that the idea of dance as constant movement and agitation is really a historic construction. He points out that the development of dance as an autonomous art form in the West, from the Renaissance onward, increasingly aligns itself with an ideal of mobility. Dance's drive toward a spectacular display of movement becomes its modernity.[31] Baker's so-called snake, giraffe, kangaroo, or monkey dances[32] thus bespeak both animalization *and* the kinetic spectacle of modernity. Her slim behind, rather than incarnating the steatopygia of the Venus Hottentot, invokes the specter of the restless modern engine.

This intimate relationship between Baker's moving body and the modern engine is already part of the vocabulary of neoclassicism that integrates the dream of modern uniformity with atavism. In the filmic poetics of *Princesse Tam Tam*, we find, for instance, this perfect union of Taylorism and neoclassical aesthetics. Let us consider these images.

The first two images (figures 7.6 and 7.7) feature the stage set and performance from the extended dance number in *Princesse Tam Tam*

Fig. 7.6

Fig. 7.7

(1935, directed by Edmond T. Gréville) that introduces Baker's climactic and supposedly revelatory strip act. The third image (figure 7.8), cited by Alan Colquhoun as an example of neoclassicism, documents a dance event staged at the Dalcroze Institute (1911–1912) in Hellerau, Germany, built by the neoclassical architect Heinrich Tessenow with a stage designed by the Swiss designer Adolphe Appia.[33] The similarities are remarkable: both performances create a close relationship between the architecture of the set and the formal patterns created by the dancers; both celebrate the intimacy between ritual and geometry; both invoke those black-and-white geometric patterns that we well recognize by now. In Gréville's production, architecture and body mime each other to the extent that the dancers' bodies (dressed

Fig. 7.8

in black-and-white patterns like the stage itself and alternately turning their bodies into patterns themselves) become architectural elements themselves.

The Dalcroze-Tessenow collaboration's relation to notions of body, movement, discipline, and German nationalism serves well to remind us of the profound historic and aesthetic affinity between atavistic ritual and modern geometric form[34] (figures 7.9, 7.10, and 7.11). Under the rubric

Fig. 7.9

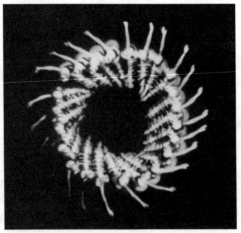

Fig. 7.10

Fig. 7.11

of neoclassicism, hedonism and discipline choreograph each other. The visual and structural affinity between Tessenow/Appia/Dalcroze and Gréville's cinematic stage further underscores the intimacy between the primitive and the exotic and the modern, technological ideals of order and discipline. If Tessenow is known to have drawn his notion of modern abstraction directly from neo-Greco motifs as Jaques-Dalcroze did from Arabic music, then we must recall that in modern dance history, we witness a similar nostalgia. Isadora Duncan, of course, comes to mind as the most apt example of the intimacy between neoclassicism, primitivist, and orientalist tropes.[35] This modernist nostalgia gets repeated in *Princesse Tam Tam* but with a twist. When we first see Alwina (Baker), she is dancing "naturally" (that is, supposedly for herself and in her own native elements), wearing a simple, Duncan-like tunic, moving among what looks like Roman ruins in war-torn Tunisia. But Baker's choreographic allusion to Duncan and the setting not only acts out the stylistic connection between archaism and its modernist revival; it also indexes the histories of imperial violence and conquest (embedded in Tunisia itself) founding that connection.

The relationship between "machine" and "animal" that Baker choreography resurrects is thus in the end a neurotic one. And here I use the term "neurosis" to signal Baker's disruption of the Taylorism that she both enacts and rejects. For if the Taylorized body is a highly disciplined body in which all waste of motion has been eliminated, then Baker's frantically moving body recalls a machine that is in disorder, a machine whose movements have exceeded its prescribed routine. It is not a coincidence that Baker first came to the attention of the impresarios as a comedian rather than a femme fatale. Critics such as Jayna Brown and Daphne Brooks have shrewdly observed that Baker made her name as a clown and that she, imitating her fellow performer Ethel Waters, would often take the position of the last girl in the chorus line, the one who is doing the "cutting up."[36] In fact, Baker played the clown as much as she played the Black Venus. In the context of our discussion, we might say that Baker upsets the "machine of girls" even as she operates as one of its cogs. Indeed, Baker's supposedly unpracticed, improvisational style is clearly a studied repudiation of the discipline that it in fact exercises.

More than simply machinelike, Baker's figure enacts the modern machine's internal struggle between ideals of human emulation and the condition of the inhuman. The modern fascination with yet fear of artificial life, what Donna Haraway would call a cyborg logic, gets played out in Baker's performative idiom: so much of Baker's choreography was, physically and rhetorically, about the pull between animation and inanimacy.[37] But in Baker's "cybernetic" performances, the terms being disrupted are not only sexual but also racial. Consider, for example, her performance in "Chocolate Dandies," an image of which we saw earlier in our study (figure 4.4). Going back to that photograph, we see Baker perched perilously on a horizontal railing, as if held up by invisible strings or secretly propped up from behind, her face in brazen minstrel makeup, her body clad in a childish dress made of checkered tablecloth material, topped by a disproportionately large bow and completed by a pair of enormous clown shoes. This image clearly draws from the minstrel tradition, as noted in chapter 4, but now we are ready to see also the allusion to Raggedy Ann, a fictional rag-doll character created by Johnny Gruelle (1880–1938) in 1915 in a series of books for young children. Baker's minstrel version of Raggedy Ann suggests that the doll, with its mop of red ropy hair, in transforming poverty, homelessness, and social waste into the source of cuddly affection, may itself carry more than a whiff of minstrel pathos. Baker's "chocolate doll" is also at once more comical and more erotic.[38] Her rubbery-legged pose appears ungainly yet unwittingly seductive, making the viewer into the supervising adult and the lecher at the same time. This figure fluctuates between a waif, a clown, and a demimondaine. In this still, we feel compressed as pure latency all the energy and antics of the performance it memorializes. Indeed, the "doll" looks as if she, finally at rest, is also just about to jump off that rail.

Compare that image to the publicity shot for the *danse sauvage* with Joe Alex (figure 4.2). That image shows Baker in her most iconographic, self-assured, self-exhibiting raw sexuality. But we might see these images, often taken as the opposite poles of Baker iconography (the waif versus the Black Venus), as in fact articulating a parable about the distilled nature of racialized female sexuality. For the *danse sauvage* also offers a parable about the tension between life and death, inanimatedness and revival. The choreography of the *danse sauvage* dramatizes a critical perversion of the definitions of mastery and enslavement. It actually tells a story in which Baker portrays the "dead" prey of a hunter played by Alex, the African native. The dance thus plays on layers of meanings: highlighting Baker's objectification as dancer (the dead weight/burden), as woman (man's prey), as Black subject (turned into object), and as American turned into the hunted by "native Africa" (represented by her partner) in a narrative reversal of American slavery. And Baker herself gets to play out on that stage the identities and the contradictions inherent in literally every term of the phrase: an exiled African American woman. The physicality of the routine also relies on the tensile relationship between weight and motion. The flights from death into life and life into death dramatized in a piece such as the *dance sauvage* not only provide the narrative basis for choreographic movements but also offer a larger parable about the racial and gender entrapments awaiting the Black female body poised between the fantasy of objecthood and the dream of animation.

The images of the "Chocolate Dandies" and of the "danse sauvage" (figures 4.1 and 4.2), taken together, offer a kind of parable, tracking a shift from an inanimate being reluctantly animated (the doll about to dance) to an animate being reluctantly becoming statuesque (the woman arrested in motion). The core of Baker's dancing in these performances draws from that which exceeds routinized or stable movement; indeed, this excess marks the special animation that is Baker dancing. We might think of Baker's especially jerky and frenetic version of the already energetic Charleston, for instance, as also archiving this tensile relationship between mechanics and biology, between form and irregularity. (This may be the perfect moment to mention that Loos, the reputed champion of order and simplicity, boasted of having learned the Charleston from Baker herself.) We may even go as far as to say that Baker choreography is often speaking to notions of waste: wasted body parts; waste of energy; the wastrel. If stylization represents ornament and excess, then there is something about Baker's choreographic style that in fact speaks directly to the value of waste.

8

All That Glitters Is Not Gold
(or, Dirty Professors)

Joséphine, a reed both dark and pale . . .

—Paul Brach

The shade of Josephine Baker's skin itself seems to waver between idealized goldenness and abject darkness. Baker herself was known to tell contradictory stories about her origin, as well as to complain that certain roles had been denied to her because she was considered either too dark or too light/"yellow."[1] Not only did her debut onstage in Paris spark debates about the status of her race, as we saw earlier, but her films also often capitalized on her racial ambiguity. In *La sirène des tropiques*, she plays the "native" daughter of the "old colonialist"; in *Zouzou*, she plays (in, I think, an uncanny anticipation of Scott McGehee and David Siegel's 1994 *Suture*) the twin of a white man played by Jean Gabin. This woman with the golden skin thus presses us to reconsider the crisis of value and its legibility as it plays out on the skin of the Black woman.

As noted, gold provides a central motif in Baker iconography. That most malleable and ductile of metals, often placed next to Baker's displayed skin, has long absorbed (like that skin) layers of social and symbolic values, and it is on the golden skin of Baker that we will now trace the fraught historic and racialized imbrications undergirding the entwined themes of *ornamentation*, *waste*, *nationhood*, and *femininity*. To fully appreciate Baker's relationship to waste and its inverse— and what it is doing to notions of style and taste in the making of the modern (and the modern nation-state)—we have to leave Baker to take in a broader view. To begin with, the association among notions

Second Skin. Second edition. Anne Anlin Cheng, Oxford University Press. © Oxford University Press 2023.
DOI: 10.1093/oso/9780197748381.003.0008

of femininity, soil, cover, and civilization is a very old one—or a very early modern one. In William Shakespeare's *The Merchant of Venice*, we find one of the more famous literary celebrations of inward beauty and worth:

> So may the outward shows be least themselves:
> The world is still deceived with ornament . . .
> Thy paleness moves me more than eloquence.[2]

These words are spoken by Bassanio, who may turn out to be the ultimate modern purist. In selecting the lead casket over the gold or the silver, Bassanio demonstrates his distaste for deceptive ornamentation and false covering and, in doing so, wins his true love. But, like Adolf Loos, the man who supposedly chooses essence over style, Bassanio is at heart a master stylist. For although the moral of the play, articulated by the scroll within the casket, insists that Bassanio succeeds because he acts "not by the view," the fact is, given the choices of three caskets identical but for their colors, Bassanio can in fact do nothing but choose by the view.

Furthermore, his taste for the styleless lead is no less a stylistic choice—indeed, a stylistic selection laden with the most nuanced, aesthetic discrimination and with ideological content:

> Thus ornament is but the guilèd shore
> To a most dangerous sea, the beauteous scarf
> Veiling an Indian beauty . . .
> . . . Therefore then, thou gaudy gold,
> Hard food for Midas, I will none of thee;
> Nor none of thee, thou pale and common drudge
> 'Tween man and man. But thou, thou meager lead
> Which rather threaten'st than dost promise aught,
> Thy paleness moves me more than eloquence.

The yellow woman signals seductive and deceptive ornamentation, while the pale woman (here "Fair Portia") whom the plain lead casket represents embodies truth and enduring value. We need not belabor the racist and sexist logics supporting this equation. Yet this logic undermines itself, for are gold and lead (and, concomitantly, yellow and fair women) so different from each other? Plain lead, we see here, is not without its own ornamental qualities. In fact, it apparently possesses a highly distinctive aesthetic characteristic: it is a most precise shade of pale. Moreover, though silent, it is at once subtle and flirtatious in its communication. Lead invokes rather than instantiates the lack of value, which is to say it is a material that leads one to reflect on the nature of value itself.

It is also the most feminized surface of the three surfaces offered, whose teasing promise of anything and nothing ("dost promise aught") is clearly associated with Portia herself, an identificatory collapse that is announced by the content in the lead casket: "Fair Portia's counterfeit!"[3] Although the word "counterfeit" in Shakespeare primarily signifies "representation in a picture, imitation," the connotation of deception and corrupted value (that is, between the copy and its original) is inevitable. According to the *Oxford English Dictionary*, a range of definitions that can support either reading has existed since circa 1590, and the authenticity of Portia's reputed virtue itself is, not surprisingly, a contested issue in Shakespearean scholarship. What concerns us here is the web of associative meanings (tying appearance to value, waste, femininity, and racial difference) being generated right there on the surface of that lead casket—and the nagging threat that gold may not be so different from lead.

It is, of course, Sigmund Freud who famously points out in his essay "The Theme of the Three Caskets" that the test of the three caskets represents a choice about three women (the Fates) and that the choice for lead is really a choice for death.[4] For Freud, the choice of death is ineluctable—an "obedience to a compulsion"—but is made bearable via reaction-formation (itself, by the way, a cover) when a wishful opposite replaces this reality; thus, "the Goddess of Death was replaced by the Goddess of Love."[5] In one sweep, Freud gives us a sequence of associations that ties femininity to objecthood ("caskets are also women"),[6] to waste (as dross and lead), and to death itself.

But whereas Freud emphasizes the aural dimension to Bassanio's choice (according to Freud, "Gold and silver are 'loud'; lead is dumb"),[7] seeing the choice as fundamentally a visual and even stylistic one helps us see the threatening lack of distinction between gold and lead.

Authenticity and its counterfeit may be more troublingly similar than not, just as the woman who holds the key to this difference is herself Janus-faced. Not only is Portia both love and death, but her figure also suggests the inseparability between veil and authenticity. After all, the woman who hides a likeness of herself in a casket is hardly unfamiliar with the play of the veil.

The question, then, is which waste covers itself better. Freud himself will tell us elsewhere that gold is itself a cover for waste (feces, to be precise). In "Anxiety and Instinctual Life," Freud links primitive instincts to excrement to precious gifts:

> Let us therefore allow ourselves to be reminded by Abraham that embryologically the anus corresponds to the primitive mouth, which has migrated down to the end of the bowel. We have learned, then, that after a person's own faeces, his excrement, has lost its value for him, this instinctual interest derived from the anal source passes over onto objects that can be presented as *gifts*. And this is rightly so, for faeces were the first gift that an infant could make, something he could part with out of love. . . . [T]his ancient interest in faeces is transformed into the high valuation of *gold* and *money* but also makes a contribution to the affective cathexis of *baby* and *penis*.[8]

On the one hand, this account tells a familiar story about civilization, its advancements and sublimations. On the other hand, it underscores the profound nostalgia that *is* the very expression of civilization, as well as highlighting the essential need of "covers" for the making of civilized values. Gold and money provide sublimated ways for us to retain rather than transcend our anal attachments, just as femininity has been enjoined to embody the sign of *lost* value, even as it facilitates the revaluation of the penis: "When a child, unwillingly enough, comes to realize that there are human creatures who do not possess a penis, that organ appears to him as something detachable from the body and becomes unmistakably analogous to the excrement."[9]

Although it is easy to dismiss Freud's phallocentric mapping from female lack to excrement to babies and penis, there is a point here about the relationship between value and nothingness that I wish to retrieve, for it is this intimate relationship that continues to serve as the foundation for aesthetic and social meanings today. Darian Leader locates the important role that absence and lack play in the making of civilized values:

> And this is why art is so expensive. . . . The art market exists as a kind of installation within civilization to remind us of what happened to make civilization possible in the first place. The gulf between money and objects is not a symptom of the art market but its condition of existence.[10]

In short, style's shallowness (its emptiness, its lack of depth or value) *is* the very evidence of and condition for its civilized value.

I go back to *The Merchant of Venice*, then, and propose that Bassanio in the end may have chosen not death, not even woman, but style/art itself. In other words, Bassanio has in fact chosen one form of excrement over another, for the real thing, so to speak, turns out to be the thing-that-needs-to-be-covered-over. Indeed, what Bassanio discovers and addresses, as if it were a person, upon opening the casket is nothing less than another cover, an image of the real: Portia-as-counterfeit. In a precursor to Loosian logic, the truly stylish woman, like fashion itself, is the one who announces herself by erasing herself, whose originality lies in her capacity to be copied and to be transferable: a paleness more moving than eloquence. This paleness, this blankness, furthermore signifies the interplay between nothing and everything that conditions the possibility of social value: "thou meager lead / Which rather threaten'st than dost promise aught." With the explosion of capitalism and commodity culture in the nineteenth and twentieth centuries, this delicate balance between worthing everything and nothing will evolve into seemingly irreconcilable opposition. (In a broad sense, Marxism is all about addressing this breakdown between object and value.) And, indeed, the valuable "paleness" that was already suggestively tainted in Shakespeare's text will transmute into the loud disquiet of the modern white surface. In short, if the racial other (the false "Oriental" in Shakespeare and the primitive in Freud) has been long recruited as a sign of waste in the golden machinery of European refinement, it is a cipher that itself brings into question the thingness and the nothingness of "pale eloquence."[11]

The questions of what is counterfeit versus authenticity, what is femininity versus masculinity, and what is decadent and in bad taste versus what is ascetic and in good taste will converge with a vengeance in Baker's film *Princesse Tam Tam*. Is Alwina the veiled yellow lady or the inert Portia? From the beginning, Alwina was labeled as waste, even manure. When Max and his colleague first saw Alwina, she was running down the street, urchinlike, in dirty bare feet. The following exchange ensues between the two French men:

MAX (LOOKING AFTER ALWINA WITH SATISFACTION): That is nature!
HIS FRIEND: I prefer perfumed chicks.
MAX (RETORTS): Nature smells better.
HIS FRIEND: Nature is manure.

On the one hand, this brief dialogue highlights the Manichaean difference between savagery and civilization on which colonialism rests. On the other hand, it also unravels the contingency upon which taste (and discrimination) is based. For if France, synecdochized in this conversation as "perfumed chicks," smells better, then "she" also embodies indigestible corporeality. After all, is not the very purpose of perfume to act fetishistically, to cover over the "real" scent of a woman? Thus, the gender difference deployed here to facilitate racial difference paradoxically unravels the nationalist pride at work here, because the project of domestication here turns out to be centered not just on the racial other but also on the (French) woman herself. To these French men, femininity must be either scatolized (as in Alwina's case) or syntheticized (as in French women). This conversation intended to debate the "naturalness" of the African other turns out to reveal a fraught anxiety about the authenticity of the French self, a national "self" that is already internally divided by sexual difference and already constituted by "waste." Value, taste, and civility: three markers of French (colonial) culture not only show themselves to be fetishized structures but also reveal their instability or, more acutely, their affinity to their opposites precisely at the contact between the West and the other.

If Max's ambition was to turn lead into gold, what he discovers is that gold may be lead after all. The "pale eloquence" of civilized values grows dark in the face of its own articulation. Consider, for example, a scene in which Max persuades Alwina to be his pupil by promising her "a pretty dress" and all the food that she can eat:

ALWINA: To get treated nicely, you have to . . . dress well?
MAX: You'll eat when you are hungry.
ALWINA (WITH GLEE): Eat when I am hungry!
MAX: Your life will become more regular. You'll eat when we eat.
ALWINA: Ah, yes, when the bell rings everyone comes to eat.
MAX: That's right.
ALWINA: What if one doesn't come? What then?
MAX: If one doesn't want to, one doesn't come.
ALWINA: Then why bother with the bell?
MAX: It's hard to explain. You learn by living with us.
ALWINA: As I understand it . . . one should be hungry when the bell rings.
MAX: That's it.
ALWINA: And if I am not hungry?
MAX: The stomach gets used to eating at mealtimes. The stomach becomes civilized. Alwina, you know, civilization is beautiful.

In this extended decoding of the semiotics of the dinner bell, we first learn that being civilized is a matter of dress and style rather than substance or essence. We are then promised civilization's gratification, which is instantaneous—that is, one gets to eat whenever one is hungry—only to learn that civilization gratifies not so much immediacy as mediation. It turns out that "instant gratification" really means training and routinization. Civilization means having one's appetites and desires conditioned in the proverbial Pavlovian exercise. As Max succinctly puts it, "the stomach becomes civilized." And if Max's dinner bell is a metaphor for the call/interpellation of civilization, then Alwina's subsequent series of inquiries unpacks the authority behind that call and demonstrates that behind civilization's contentment lie the specter and discipline of discontentment/hunger.

The very teaching of civilization in this exchange displays its own pedagogical necessity. The teacher, too, has had to be trained. (This is why haute cuisine retains the marks of savagery, for who is more sophisticated in his or her savagery than the gourmand? Delicacies such as *les escargots, los pesques mejillas, le foie de canard, le boudin,* and more boast of an exclusivity that is so precisely because of its patience for courting the earthy and the visceral.) If Africa represents "natural manure," then colonial France is but raw material that has learned to announce its renunciations. Max's final words above ("Alwina, you know, civilization is beautiful") reveal that the aestheticization of discipline *is* the education of desire. It is not just a question of what to wear or how to eat but the apprehension of the *pleasure of self-management* that marks the civilized master.

This self-management—obviously growing out of an anxiety about bodily waste—enjoys an enduring presence in not only modern aesthetic value but also the ideological construction of the modern nation-state, both Western and non-Western. This accounts for the ubiquity of lavatory discussions in the most surprising of texts. In 1933, the great Japanese novelist Junichiro Tanizaki wrote a gorgeous, slim volume on the principle of traditional Japanese architecture and its relation to modern Japanese national identity:

> The Japanese toilet truly is a place of spiritual repose. . . . There are certain prerequisites: a degree of dimness, absolute cleanliness, and a quiet so complete one can hear the hum of a mosquito. . . . What need is there to remind us so forcefully of the issue of our own bodies[?] . . . How crude and tasteless to expose the toilet to . . . excessive illumination. . . . The cleanliness of what can be seen only calls up the more clearly thoughts of what cannot be seen. . . . There is no denying, at any rate, that among the elements of the elegance in which we take such delight is a measure of the unclean, the insanitary. But we Orientals . . . create a kind of beauty of the shadows we have made in out-of-the-way places. . . . Were it not for shadows, there would be no beauty.[12]

In Praise of Shadows opens with this lyrical meditation on the premodern, nonelectric Japanese lavatory, claiming for this space of privacy incomparable spiritual repose and the precious reserve of last shadows. By drawing a direct analogy between Japanese national character and aesthetic principles in Japanese architecture and design, Tanizaki argues and mourns for a style/character that is rapidly passing away in the face of rampant modernization, that is to say, westernization. But this praise of darkness is riddled with paradoxes. Is this passage an example of Oriental decadence or ascetic repose? How can "absolute cleanliness" be reconciled with "a measure of uncleanliness"? How can darkness enable illumination? Why go to the toilet at all as the site for redeeming the (national and personal) body?

Tanizaki's turn to the toilet is not at all idiosyncratic when we consider how the toilet has been (pardon the pun) the seat for imagining Western civilization. Freud is well known for suggesting that civilization is built on the repression of the scatological. In *Civilization and Its Discontents*, he famously claims that when men walked on all fours, smell was the most important sense, but when they stood erect, vision became privileged and the olfactory and the excremental at once degraded and repressed.[13] The cultural trend toward cleanliness is thus directly linked to civilization, progress, and vision. As Anne McClintock has eloquently argued, the ideal of cleanliness constitutes a powerful and complex tool of colonial ideology and imperial dissemination.[14] And, as we have seen via thinkers such as Loos and Le Corbusier, the ideology of cleanliness and the movement toward deornamentation sustained the making of a modern and implicitly European style. Tanizaki's treatise may even be seen as a direct rebuttal of Le Corbusier's proclamation for Western cleanliness. Consider Le Corbusier's seminal essay "A Coat of Whitewash; the Law of Ripolin," written some eight years prior to *In Praise of Shadows*:

> Imagine the results of the Law of Ripolin. Every citizen is required to replace his hangings, his damasks, his wall-papers, his stencils, with a plain coat of white ripolin. His home is made clean. There are no more dirty, dark corners. Everything is shown as it is. Then comes inner cleanness, for the course adopted leads to refusal to allow anything at all which is not correct, authorized, intended, desired, thought-out. . . . When you are surrounded with shadows and dark corners . . . [y]ou are no master in your own house. Once you have put ripolin on your walls you will be master of yourself.[15]

It would seem that Tanizaki's words aimed to reclaim and purify those "dirty, dark corners" so imperiously rejected by Le Corbusier.

We can also trace another potential interlocutor for Tanizaki: an 1898 essay by Loos, appropriately titled "Plumbers," where we find an ardent praise of English toilets, spigots, and water. In what might be called without hyperbole Loos's song of the toilets, we find a wittily ironic but serious Loos linking personal hygiene directly to (European) national character and health:

> There would be no nineteenth century without the plumber. . . . [T]he plumber is the pioneer of cleanliness. He is the state's chief craftsman, the quartermaster of culture. . . . Every English washbasin with its spigot and drain is a marvel of progress.[16]

It is in this same article that Loos reminds us that the word "plumber" is not English or German but borrowed from the Latin word *plumbum*, meaning lead. (Can we call Shakespeare's Bassanio not only the protopurist but also the protoplumber?) All these men of hygiene, however, turn out to be as preoccupied with what the lavatory maintains as with what it expunges. This staged exchange among Tanizaki, Le Corbusier, and Loos shows not their explicit nationalist competitiveness but their similarities: all three espouse the values of frankness, deornamentation, and cleanliness (even if defined differently), and all three share a fundamental anxiety about the threatening prospect of (bodily, national, and racial) shame.

In fact, the specter of the soiled body proves to be the most resistant object for all three writers. Hal Foster has traced Loos's work on ornament to Freud's work on excrement as complementary narratives about the progress of individuals and civilization that turn on the anal. As Foster points out, the crime of the ornament, for Loos, is that it is excremental.[17] He locates in Loos a profound anxiety about anal contamination; in short, Loos responds to that anxiety about anal contagion by becoming an anal character. Let me add here that this "anal character" is specifically also an anxious national character:

> Germany needs a good bath. . . . We really do not need art at all. . . . We need culture. . . . Next to the academies we should build baths, and along with the professors we should appoint bath attendants.

> May our Viennese plumbers fulfill their task and bring us to that important goal, the attainment of a cultural level equal to the rest of the civilized Western world. For otherwise, something very unpleasant, very shameful could happen to us. Otherwise, if both nations continue to progress at their present rate, the Japanese could attain Germanic culture before the Austrians do.[18]

Plumbers are equal, indeed, preferable, to professors. (Here how can we not think of Max de Mirecourt, the dirty professor who gives elegant lessons in stomach management but who really prefers the smell of manure?) Plumbers are, after all, the architects of modern hygiene. And modern hygiene in turn provides the foundation for modern nationhood. Moreover, we should note that the national character that Loos is speaking of is really Austrian. Hence, Austrians can become more German by way of becoming more English and not to be outdone by the Japanese. In short, behind the German body lies the shameful Austrian body.

We can detect a similar anxiety in Le Corbusier's Ripolin essay, where the "ideal body" is one that must be cleaned up and painted over in order to be a proper Western, civilized body—a compulsion that betrays the pressing encroachment of "shadows and dark" that would threaten the unseemly loss of self-control: "you are no master in your own house." It is even more telling that this essay celebrating—indeed, decreeing—whiteness should repeatedly invoke its constitutive darkness: "The white of whitewash is absolute . . . everything stands out from it and is recorded absolutely, black on white; it is honest and dependable."[19] The visual examples Le Corbusier selects to represent "absolute beauty" turn out to be not pure white at all: first, a photograph of a stark black-and-white studio he designed with his cousin Pierre Jeanneret for the French cubist painter Amédée Ozenfant and, second, a photograph of the "Sultan Mahembe and his two sons" standing against a bright white sky.[20] For both Loos and Le Corbusier, these moments of purist, nationalist/aesthetic claims are punctuated by shadows of their inverse.

For Tanizaki, too, his dream of a modern Japanese nationalism separate from Western influences is continually contaminated by visions of the irredeemable soiled/dark body. Looking back to Tanizaki's text, it becomes clear that his celebration of the non-Western body in all its irreducible materiality involves, ironically, a bid for its very erasure: "[W]hat need is there to remind us so forcefully of the issue of our own bodies?" Tanizaki's call for the return to the body is thus also a turn away from the body, a contradiction that has much to do with the indigestible darkness that Tanizaki projects on "Oriental skin":

> Taken individually there are Japanese who are whiter than Westerners and Westerners who are darker than the Japanese, but their whiteness and darkness is not the same. . . . [At a party] among the Japanese there were ladies dressed in gowns no less splendid than the foreigners, and whose skin was whiter than theirs. Yet . . . the Japanese complexion, no matter how white, is tinged by a slight cloudiness. These women were in no way reticent about powdering themselves. Every bit of exposed flesh . . . they cover with a thick coat of white. Still they cannot efface the darkness that lay below their skin. It was as plainly visible as dirt at the bottom of a pool of pure water.[21]

This passage is fascinating in so many ways, not the least of which is the implicit transmutation of Le Corbusier's "thick coat of white" into the makeup on the faces of Japanese women. But has Tanizaki transformed or repeated the logic of that "coat of white"?

For if we have come to understand by now the "thick coat of white" of modern, Western architectural theory as an articulation rather than disavowal of its nostalgia for dark skins, then Tanizaki's painted women here equally announce "yellow skin's" longing for whiteness. This is why this song of shadows is also so fundamentally melancholic, because it is being sung from a place of self-rejection. Tanizaki's house of literature, his chosen last haven for resistance against the encroachment of westernization, retains "Oriental darkness" with utter ambivalence:

> But we must be resigned to the fact that as long as *our skin is the color it is* the loss we have suffered cannot be remedied. . . . I would call back at least for literature this world of shadows we are losing. In this mansion called literature I would have the eaves deep and the walls

dark, *I would push back into the shadows the things that come forward
too clearly, I would strip away the useless decoration.* . . . [P]erhaps we
may be allowed at least one mansion where we can turn off the electric lights and see what it is like without them.[22]

Skin color thus operates like a tattoo, a mark of regression that cannot
be erased. Part of what lends this song of darkness its poignancy is how
it has inherited the vocabulary of the ideological-aesthetic complex
against which it pushes.

By celebrating denuded darkness as the privileged aesthetic-ethical
form, Tanizaki explicitly transforms Western Enlightenment, symbolized
by electricity, into that which is superfluous and deceptive, but he has
also implicitly reiterated its ideological attachment to "pale eloquence."
The world of shadowed beauty that Tanizaki wishes to preserve is in
fact being retroactively created by him as the negative image of Western
racial discourse about Oriental tarnish. Tanizaki's restful mansion is
thus also a tomb, a place of mourning. The refuge of Japanese letters
and arts therefore offers not a respite but a safe house within which
the inescapable melancholy of "Oriental taint" would be not so much
dispelled as nursed.

Some sixty years later in another meditation on the play of shadow
and light, Toni Morrison would speak of the unspoken yet constitutive presence of Blackness in American literature.[23] In Tanizaki's case,
we might say we are witnessing the unspoken but constitutive presence of whiteness in Japanese shadows. In short, Tanizaki's project
of deornamentation and de-westernization paradoxically entails a
project of self-marking.[24] The melancholy of Tanizaki's project and its
internal paradoxes derive from the fact that this praise of shadows is
itself shadowed by an anxiety about the body's irredeemable otherness.

Finally, it is significant that the idea of a racial taint is most visibly
located by Tanizaki on the surface of *female* skin (as dirt, shadow,
and waste). For Le Corbusier, too, the conspicuous absence of female
bodies announces itself in the "dirty, dark corners" and enveloping
"shadows" that "man" must "master" in order to master himself. The
shared "ghost in the machine," to borrow Morrison's words, of this
nexus of texts by Tanizaki, Loos, and Le Corbusier is the haunting
specter of the soiled body and, especially, that of the soiled, nonwhite,

female body. The veiled lady—dark, muddy, and orientalized—is as in-digestible to Loos's and Le Corbusier's narratives of Western progress as it is to Tanizaki's utopian dream of an alternative Eastern modernity.

At last we return to Baker. If the historic and literary specters of Portia-as-lead and yellow-woman-as-mud raise the question of whether femininity is an inert or active surface, shallow or full of con-tent, then Baker-as-gold suggests a profound and multiple engagement with the notions of value and style at the convergence of literary and colonial history, psychoanalytic discourse, and modernist aesthetics. Her golden-yet-soiled body, instead of simply representing the site of national indigestibility, actually launches the *crisis* of value engendered by imperial desire. We can juxtapose Baker next to the shadows of Tanizaki's muddy, yellow woman, bringing into full view the rela-tion between primitivism and orientalism that ties both concepts to the making of an ideal modern surface/skin. That is, our discussions of primitivism must expand to include its twin, orientalism, and how both discursive and imaginative practices inform the making of Western aesthetic theory in ways well beyond that of providing a contrast.

Indeed, it is through this interconnection among ideas of waste, nationhood, and racialized femininity that we see how central the concept of orientalism is to both the discourse of primitivism and European refinement. It is not a mere coincidence that Baker, the quin-tessentially primitivist figure, should be *also* frequently orientalized. Consider, for instance, the Siberian tiger with whom she is often juxtaposed and compared, her pairing with Oceanic as well as African artifacts in photographs, and so forth. This association is especially pronounced in *Princesse Tam Tam*: the name Alwina is Arabic; Baker/Alwina is diegetically, symbolically, and even sartorially linked to the mysterious Maharajah. Indeed, Alwina's final return to Tunisia and the Blackness it connotes is mysteriously narrated by the Maharajah as a return toward the East. We can say that the conflation of primitivism and orientalism is but a symptom of general Western racism: both serve colonial desire; both share the trope of feminized skin as a site of fetishization and waste. But there is a distinctive difference between how these two discourses formulate their visions of racialized female skin: one is about exposure and the other about covering. That is, the primitive Black woman is all about exposed nakedness, while the "Oriental" woman is all about sartorial excess, the excessive covering and ornamentation that supposedly symptomize the East's overly developed, effeminized, corrupt, and declining civilization. Compare, for instance, the popularized image of Saartjie "Sarah" Baartman (1789–1815), also known as the Venus Hottentot (figure 8.1), with the image of the overly fussily dressed "Chinese Lady" Afong Moy (1815–?),

Fig. 8.1

on display through the late nineteenth century on the circus route in America (figure 8.2).[25]

Where Baartman was stripped down for the white male gaze, the demure Moy was fully clothed and sat, herself ornament-like, among layers (tablecloths, draperies, paintings, panels, and so on) of Victorian fantasies of Chinese decorations. There is, in fact, a long-standing intimacy between the discourse of nineteenth-century European

Fig. 8.2

decadence and orientalism, often signaled by an excessive preoccupa-
tion with fabrics. (Consider, for example, the obsession with textile in
Joris-Karl Huysmans's classic novel of European decadence, *Against
Nature [Á rebours]*, 1884.)

The tropes of primitive nakedness and encrusted, sartorial,
Oriental decadence, of course, come together to exoticize and objectify the non-Western, racial other. Yet what is interesting about
Baker is the ways in which she makes the conditions of nakedness
and waste *equivalent to* the conditions of sartorial excess in such a
way as to unravel values underlying these stylistic and ideological
categories. We observed earlier how Baker's unrevealing strip act
in *Princesse Tam Tam* plays on the interchangeability of skin and
cloth, a complication that not only reveals colonial fetishism's built-
in failure but also deeply troubles notions of racialized embodiment
in contemporary progressive discourse. Now we can go further and
add that Baker's movement from shining goldenness to supposedly
abject Blackness entails not a transformation but an enactment of
the fundamental doubleness founding colonial value, especially at
the site of the raced body. *Gold and manure show their equivalence.*
In the climactic scene of performance in *Princesse Tam Tam*, Baker
goes from gold to blackness. Yet she has not so much stripped or
degenerated as she has crystallized and unveiled the very history of
the "black gold" that fed the slave trade from the west coast of Africa
across the Atlantic. What constitutes gold versus dross, just as what
constitutes taste versus distaste, gets turned upside down—or,
rather, inside out. We see, literally, the mask of Blackness founding
the possibility of gold.

Princesse Tam Tam—a film in which Baker plays an incarnation of
common trash turned royalty turned trash again, and in which such a
transformation of value is meant to reveal the nature of essentialized
Blackness and civilized Frenchness—thus speaks to the larger and
more fraught transnational history in the making of material value
based on human bodies. As Saidiya Hartman points out,

> Before Sigmund Freud detailed the symbolic affinities between gold
> and excrement, African royals were stockpiling their gold in privies
> and selling slaves for chamber pots. (And European traders were

transforming humans into waste and back again through the exchange of gold.)[26]

The gold that sheathes Baker's body in the film operates as cipher and
citation: not only of the currency of European civilized refinement but
also of the discourses of psychoanalysis on fetishism; the history of
"black gold" in the transatlantic slave trade; the philosophic association
of femininity with inert surfaces; and modernism's larger philosophic
argument about ornamentation in fields from art to architecture.

The question of style is thus far from incidental but proves to be
central to the project of nation making. Taste—itself perhaps the cornerstone of fetishistic preference—offers an aesthetic linchpin in the
colonial and modern political imagination. It is the very thing that
Max tries to impart to Alwina in their sessions, and it is the revelation of taste, or lack thereof, that supposedly exposes Alwina in the
end, but we already know that good taste in *Princesse Tam Tam* has a
tendency to show its profound bad taste. Indeed, alongside the theme
of waste, the question of style becomes an increasingly pressing preoccupation of the film, both diegetically and cinematographically. At the
level of plot, the more Alwina labors to naturalize herself into civilized
style, the more artificial and extraneous that style appears. And this
is not only because the film wants ultimately to exclude Alwina from
that style but also because that style *must be* denaturalized in order to
be recognized *as* style, that is, as a contrast against and a compensation for the naked, atavistic body. Thus, Max's elegant, bright, white
Parisian apartment is a study in modern simplicity, a simplicity that, of
course, fulfills itself through accessories: streamlined furniture, artificial flowers, a fake fish congealed in a bowl.

At the level of cinematography, however, style desires anything but
naturalism. If French style is being deconstructed as mass-produced,
derivative, even deadly, the film itself celebrates the other aspects of
modernism: technology, inorganic animation, reproduction. And
if Max is finally saved from the failure of his fetishistic desire,[27] we
the viewers are not allowed similar respites (whereby colonial authority is conserved after its ruptures) because our eyes have already
been seduced by a highly miscegenated style that compels us and
keeps us happy in our disorder. I am referring to how the style of the

cinematography, precisely at the moment when Alwina is being outed in that dance sequence, actively dislocates us and gives us pleasure in that dislocation. To remind us, Alwina's supposed primitive self-exposure is nestled within a much longer musical and dance sequence, replete with Chinese acrobats, African drummers, and dancers both exotic and French: a wild collage befitting the theme of exotic abandonment. Viewers will, however, also remember that this elaborate and extended dance number which frames and erupts between Baker's own choreography is shamelessly in love with displaying what the camera can do: jump cuts, splices, special camera lenses, and more. This highly visual sequence paradoxically disrupts vision. It also relentlessly foregrounds the mechanism, technologies, and modes of seeing.

Much earlier we observed that a different kind of looking became necessary when cinema came into being. Here we have a vibrant example of how the human eye gets manipulated and distorted by cinematic style. In this sequence, we are constantly trying to adjust our eyes to shifting lenses and levels of reality. Aesthetically, on the level of surface (forms and colors), the sequence is vertiginous. We are shown multiple layers of dizzying black-and-white geometric patterns: on the stage, on the props (like the chessboard that expands to become the stage at one point), on the dancers' costumes, on the patterns made by the dancers' bodies themselves (figure 8.3).

Narratively, we are also thrown because the levels of reality and physical space shift, dissolve, and collide. Stages within stages dissolve, layer over, or expand into one another; scales of things change dramatically; so that the "stages" that we the film viewers see cannot possibly be the same stage as that which the diegetic nightclub audience sees. Even the real bodies onstage highlight their dizzying compatibility with the unreal; for instance, the chorines' synchronized bodies twirl and transform, through dissolve effect, into dolls on the spinning black-and-white plates of the mysterious Chinese acrobats, themselves suggesting the coincidence of exotic, folk performance and the modern language of mechanical precision. This is to say, we have a scene of Taylorism at its most rationalized madness: a compulsion (to borrow Fleissner's word) poised on the brink between uncontrollable madness and utter discipline.

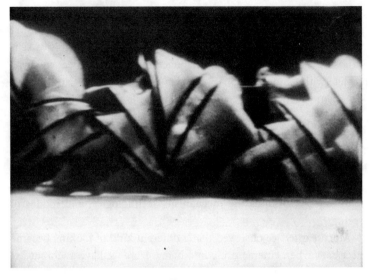

Fig. 8.3

And our eyes are irrevocably recruited by the making of this dream. Contrary to the assumption that the movie theater maintains the integrity of the viewing subject (he or she gets to sit anonymously in the dark), the cinema not only actually enlists the body of its viewer at the level of fantasy (hence so much of early film theory compares film spectatorship to dreaming) but also co-opts and reorganizes that body as a mode of production. As Jonathan Beller eloquently puts it, "Cinema brings the industrial revolution to the eye, and engages spectators in increasingly dematerialized processes of social production."[28] For Beller, cinema extends the logic of the assembly line, a claim that holds wide-ranging implications for the commodification of vision and subjectivity. I want to take a more modest, even literalist, point from his broader insight, which is to understand the technologicalization of the human eye: that the eye enters not only into labor but into technology itself, which in turn means entering into a new plasticity of time and space. In *Princesse Tam Tam*, we experience precisely the convergence of visual labor, technology, and pleasure. That is, social production translates into affective pleasure, and affective pleasure articulates itself through social production. In the crucial sequence framing Baker's finale, the camera filters through a kaleidoscopic lens, creating multiple and repetitive framed shots in geometric patterns (figures 7.9–7.11). If this scene of metadisplay turns the viewer into the voyeur, the camera with its refracted views also makes insects or machines out of its audience. That is, the viewer's own viewing experience becomes other-than-human. Technical euphoria is thus not seen as a triumph against or an observation of but as a dynamic companion to, if not the very vehicle for, feminine and atavistic passions. Hence the jungle heartbeats of the drums *are* echoed by the techniques of serial jump cuts. Hence the fragmentation of body parts *partakes* of the pleasure of cinematic possibilities. Instead of corporeal exposure or even presence, what we get is the hedonism of stylistic reproduction.

Opting for this stylistic jouissance, the film is perfectly willing to sacrifice its realism. This says something about the willful fantasy of colonial imagination, but it also says something about how the imaginative driven by modern technology might undermine the desire for the real driving ethnographic conquest. Instead of thinking about cinema as a medium for enabling touristic or ethnographic information, critic Katherine Groo has made the observation that ethnographers come to reject cinematic representation because of the genre's instability.[29] As she points out, in *Princesse Tam Tam* and in the highly extravagant and consciously dreamlike sequence that has been occupying our attention, there are segments of ethnographic documentaries that have been spliced in but such an unrealistic way as to render the importation pronounced. There is, for example, the shot of what appears to be a West African drummer playing on a *dundun* drum but who clearly was not on the physical stage of the set. In short, we are looking less at an ethnographic piece disguised as fiction than at its inverse: a highly staged and artificial cinematic world that has come to swallow the ethnographic and its imagined real.

Baker-as-Alwina embodies less the ethnographic and more the cinematic. Her dance in that climactic scene is inextricably woven into the texture of the cinematography. Her body movements and the camera's (from jump cuts to panning) form a choreographic rhythm (figure 8.4).

Baker's solo performance, which is staged as an interruption, is indeed a break in the sequence, but *not* because she disrupts the Taylorized fantasy in this sequence by offering the contrast of a "real

Fig. 8.4

Black body" or a "real pagan dance" as a critique of the body-machine. Instead, she breaks the sequence by making apparent—indeed, *by performing*—style's fundamental susceptibility to contamination. In other words, the content of the diegesis may be offering us an ethnographic body, but the language of the film (the mise-en-scène, the cut, the texture of images) decenters that promise and seduces the viewer into an alternative pleasure that finds itself in film technology and *its* potential to draw the traces of human subjectivity.

Instead of revealing (national or racial) taste, we receive the crosscurrents that make up those distinctions in the first place. Baker's supposedly African and primitive choreographic diction in fact enacts a collage of South American beat and jazz, hints of Martha Graham (already a borrowing of neo-Greco classicism as well as of African and Asian choreographic rhetoric), and Caribbean and Latin American dancing, as well as the Charleston and the cakewalk, the latter two being themselves the products of cross-racial parodies in the American South.[30] This scene of discrimination is thus, significantly, a scene of stylistic indiscrimination. To "see" Baker in this number means, literally, to see her as *counterfeit*. The only "authentic" thing we can locate in this performance-within-performance is the virtuosity of movement itself. And virtuosity, instead of signaling a language of universality, speaks rather in the language of fragmentation and hybridity. Baker's moving body gives us neither harmony nor originality but citation and disarticulation. (We, for example, notice gestures to Martha Graham and the early development of modern dance with its emphasis on figural isolation.) We have the pleasures of rearticulation: an articulation of the lack of essence.

In light of the history of the persistent corporealization of the Black female body (e.g., the Venus Hottentot), Baker's fluid disarticulation of body parts generates more political impact than any claims to intention or agency in the traditional sense. The fact is, her performance is itself enacting a historic engagement—one that demands we reconsider how race, gender, body, and nationhood get staged and recognized and, quite literally, rendered visible/legible by film. Indeed, as we observed, one of the more "decadent" or sensual aspects of this final dance number has much to do with the way it has been staged and shot. The edit-and-dissolve shots used throughout the sequence effect a kind of visual blending whereby bodies and body parts slide and merge into one another, making the distinction of bodies and body parts impossible—as if the scene is itself already performing a kind of miscegenation. We can, of course, see this melding of bodies as a kind of visual realization of colonial authority's confused fantasies of primitivism, but this fusion has another performative effect on the notion of national taste.

If the dark woman is other-to-the-nation (as Loos, Le Corbusier, Shakespeare, and Tanizaki argued), then Baker shows us that the most dangerous and powerful aspect of her performance might be its suggestion that style, for all its claims to distinctiveness, is highly susceptible to contamination. French civilization, like the perfumed woman, is shown in the end to be a fragile coating not because it cannot impart its lessons to the primitive other, but because civilization exists *as* veneer. Civilization is style itself. And, as such, it is what enables the transformation of nothingness into value, dross into gold. As the character Alwina literally moves from glitter to filth, she dramatizes the profound intimacy, rather than difference, between the golden and the blackened. And the obscene (at least, for the colonial master) revelation of this sameness between gold and filth itself indexes the traumatic historical connections among human bodies, commodity value, and cross-racial negotiation behind the origins of the very term "fetishism"—itself, as William Pietz so eloquently laid out, a term born out of the conflict of value and its compensations in the early encounters between Portuguese traders and the so-called natives on the Gold Coast in the sixteenth century.[31]

Taste, then, is indeed the key, not to national or racial difference but to *the production of a dream of embodiment*. And this embodiment is built not on authentic corporeality but on the citationality of style. If the endgame of the story of the modern object, distilled from architectural theory and its attachment to the purified look of the anonymous facade, is about erasing the bad (and dark) taste of materiality to cleanse the body and to liberate the eye toward the shine of rational thought,[32] then we have to see the naked Baker as the implosion of, rather than a backdrop for, that fantasy.

If this book has seemed to eschew the question of Baker's so-called interiority, it is not only because that interiority is inaccessible to us but also because it is precisely her surface quality that collapses the difference between person and representation and, in doing so, critiques the assumption of authenticity and embodiment utilized by *both* liberal criticism and colonial racism. There is much in Baker's biography to suggest that this was an intelligent woman who lived a spectacularly public life and who lived that public life with a fair amount of insight and irony at a time when women, certainly women of color, were rarely afforded the luxury of irony. At the same time, biography is so frequently mistaken for "subjectivity," just as agency is so often redeemed at the expense of complexity, that this project has been moved to refocus our attention on the surface of Baker's art in order to attend to and rethink the terms of *its* agency. What Baker bequeaths to us is the play of her sartorial skin. And our response to the call of that seduction must be an attention to what it is saying about the lure of the surface and to the implications, at once inhibiting and generative, for grounding politics on the terms of the visible.

The unabashed lure of the surface, epitomized by Baker's performance idiom, diffuses rather than consolidates racial difference. Indeed, the most unsettling yet powerful aspect of this performance might be its suggestion that style, for all its claims to distinctiveness, is highly susceptible to contamination. Baker's performance reminds us that race, ethnicity, and nationalism enter into choreography as denotative movements, as stylistic allusions. This susceptibility, furthermore, may prove to be style's vital contribution to political engagement, for it suggests that cross-fertilization is the inevitable outcome of cross-cultural engagement. Similarly, we might say in the encounter between the West and its others, difference enters as form. How we know someone relies fundamentally on a formal process of discernment and differentiation, just as how we see ourselves depends on repeated forms of ourselves. In this sense, the other will always remain "other" and "exotic" to us. But to see this limitation built into the politics of recognition is also to acknowledge our openness to alterity— and it is that vulnerability that style's promiscuity unveils.

Baker's "primitivist" performance can only be the enactment of the doubleness of the performance of authenticity for the diasporic subject. The "call of Africa" in this scene must pose for the exiled and expatriate Baker a complicated invitation not only because the Africa being offered here is a white fantasy but also because Africa must itself be a fantasy for Baker. Baker's performance does not recuperate, but instead exposes, the Black subject as alienation. The only authentic thing we can locate in this performance is the virtuosity of movement—a virtuosity that does not allow Baker to transcend racial, gender, or national differences but that, counterintuitively, precisely reveals those distinctions to be built on transferable disembodiment and disarticulation. For Baker, the "fact of Blackness" acts as cladding—one that is neither pure illusion nor authentic embodiment but a complicated and unceasing negotiation between the two.

9
Ethical Looking

The visual culture surrounding the racialized, female body, understood to be one of the most pernicious examples of masculinist, colonial imagination, also tells alternative stories about the intersection of
power, shame, and exhibition. We have begun to locate these alternative stories by attending to the utterances left on the surfaces of Black
bodies and white buildings. From Adolf Loos's ideal of unadorned
surfaces to Baker's theatrical, layered nudity to Le Corbusier's praise of
the free facade, "modern nakedness" in fact designates not the freedom
from reprehensible distractions but the fantasy of a self-erasing mask
that is always added on and worn. And if the modernist reverence for
the transparency of surface has revealed itself to be a thin story, then
Baker's iconography shows us just how "thick" the idea of nakedness
can be.

The crystallization of "surface" as an aesthetic ideal at the birth
of the twentieth century holds profound philosophic and material
connections to (not just disavowals of) the violent and dysphoric
history of racialized, ruptured skin. Yes, the taking in of the other in
order to consolidate the self has obviously invidious potentials, but
such intaking is also when an unlikely and radical receptivity opens
up, what I elsewhere called the melancholic logic of racial identification.[1] At the same time, how racialized skin responds to relentless
corporealization and objectification may take unexpected forms. The
desire to remake oneself as object can be shared by those we think
would be most allergic to such transformation. Individuation and personhood for the objectified subject may not always take the forms of
exercising power and agency in the traditional sense but may instead
be achieved through self-evacuation as well as self-syntheticization.

Trying to house and display Baker's corporeal body led Loos to
an intricate, conceptual engagement with the very notion of abstraction, a confrontation that pushes back on the pressure points in

Second Skin. Second edition. Anne Anlin Cheng, Oxford University Press. © Oxford University Press 2023.
DOI: 10.1093/oso/9780197748381.003.0009

his own theoretical work, as well as highlighting the intricacies and contradictions inhering in ideas of racial and sexual identities. Offering up her "primitive nakedness" to the world, Baker wraps herself with an early-century imagination about and rhetoric of plasticity and cladding. In short, the story of modern abstraction, so often thought to be about purification, reveals itself to be active expressions of a fantasy of embodiment, and the story of intractable, racialized corporeality turns out to draw from—perhaps even rely on—the play and pleasures of abstraction. Alongside acts of greed, misrecognition, and borrowing, the subjects and objects of primitivist modernism (both the modernists and Baker herself) also immersed themselves in skins that were not their own and constructed themselves as imagined subjects through that inhabitation: a mutual pedagogy of erotics.

If, as I have been suggesting, racial contamination provides the precondition and expression of modern style itself, then reading "race" at the site of the most racialized performance demands that we reconsider what constitutes the terms of the visible, as well as altering how we think about the seductions, effects, and materiality of racialized skin on display. Reapproaching Baker has dictated what I call a hermeneutics of susceptibility, for it is only in allowing ourselves to remain open to the contaminated intersection of Baker's and the modernists' fantasies (those curious dreams of personhood that derive from inhabiting the skin of the other or the self-as-other) that we can begin to see not only primitivist modernism's complex realignment of subjecthood and objecthood but also its enduring challenge for contemporary critical practice.

While Baker is a unique figure born out of a particular intersection of historic and aesthetic formations, her performances speak directly to a politics of vision whose limitations continue to press upon us with ever-increasing urgency. In spite of our political sophistication today, we still have few tools and little language for addressing what I call visual pleasure in the contaminated zone: those uneasy places of visual exchange where pleasure, law, and resistance converge. From skin to surface to dynamic superficiality, reading Baker has required that we go beyond the established terms of racial visibility, underscoring how the rhetoric of "becoming visible" that has energized so much of progressive racial politics often elides the contradictions underpinning social visibility and remains inadequate to address the phenomenological, social, and psychical implications inhering in what it means *to be visible*.

As Martin Jay has reminded us, Western culture has long been thought to be highly ocular-centric; its philosophical tradition, from Plato to Jacques Lacan, has in fact harbored a deep suspicion, even denigration, of the realm of the visual and, by implication, the superficial. Today the moral economy of the visual continues to exert its pull. Especially when it comes to representations of women and racial minorities, the visual is almost always negatively inflected and usually seen as a tool of commoditization and objectification.[2] It is not a coincidence that in fields such as African American studies and African diasporic studies, the locus of revolutionary possibility often gets located in sound/music, while the visual remains a less than productive arena.[3] And where the visual does get recuperated by liberal rhetoric, it seems limited to gestures of idealization or authentication. If, as all good feminist and film theories—indeed, arguably, a whole history of Western philosophical discourse—tell us, the realm of the ocular is highly suspicious, prone to deception and reification, then what can an ethical position for both the viewer and the producer of visual images look like?

Studying Baker, we have had to ask, what are the visual conditions under which a (raced and gendered) body comes into visibility at all? What is at stake here is the very status of the racial sign: how we recognize it, how we confer or rescind value. These issues touch on the very fiber of how we imagine the psychological, social, and even legal basis for forging identity and its concomitant rights. The crisis of visuality that I have been exploring holds reaching implications for the politics of equality today. Civil rights today in America, for instance, continue to rely on the distinction between essence and performance, between being and behavior. Legal scholar Kenji Yoshino reminds us that antidiscrimination laws today are specifically based on the protection of what are understood to be immutable traits (blood, chromosome, skin color). They do not protect what are thought to be mutable or superficial characteristics (behavior, style, cultural practice). Thus, for example, in certain states, an individual cannot be fired for being Black or gay, but even within that protection, one can be fired for wearing cornrows or for "flaunting" one's gay marriage. And for Yoshino, one of the tasks for formulating the new civil rights must be the freedom to exercise one's vision of one's sense of authenticity, the right to self-fashioning.[4]

This call for authenticity, social visibility, and self-making is, of course, enormously appealing for anyone who has enjoyed none of these. But the history of the delineation of racialized bodies that we have been studying here suggests that something more fraught is at stake here than notions of authenticity—or of suppressed or ineluctable visibility, for that matter. At the beginning of this study, I raised the quandary of a binaristic racial discourse shared, surprisingly, by both colonial thinking and critical race theory. We are now in a much better position to understand the full implications of that problem. Critical race theory has taught us very persuasively that phenomena such as passing and its more contemporary version, covering, have everything to do with the unequal assignation of social and economic privileges and are symptomatic of a nation and a legal system unable to guarantee true equality. But even as critical race theory has done the vital work of unraveling racial assumptions as entirely socialized and juridicized concepts, somehow the "fact" of Blackness continues to signify unproblematically. Thus, we find, for instance, in Cheryl I. Harris's foundational essay "Whiteness as Property," an elegant exposition on how social privilege and subordination are structured on entwined concepts of race and property. Harris undoes the "fact" of whiteness. Yet the "fact" of Blackness reconstitutes itself in the essay in the form of a longing for Black authenticity, symbolized by Harris's mournful nostalgia for her grandmother who spent her life passing as white.[5]

What I am trying to point out here is that the solution of an "unmasked self" cannot be the solution to the problem of racism or discrimination, for that ideal elides how the (racialized) "self" is always already an effect of the mask worn. The dream of subjectivity has always been but an identity effect. And the question is, how does our law and can the language of civil rights accommodate the profundity and the dilemmas of this insight?

One of the most insidious consequences of prejudice has always seemed to me to be less the suppression of an authentic self than the compromise of subjective integrity effected by such discrimination in the first place. This is not to deny the importance of authenticity as an ideal or as a necessary fiction. But, like all ruling or originary fantasies we have about ourselves, these fictions are at once tenacious and fragile, insistent and susceptible. This is why "subjective agency" is at once so valuable and so vexed a notion for an individual who is already suffering under the violence of a compromised individuality. Indeed, to return to Yoshino's haunting text, the most stirring aspects of that book are precisely those moments when the narrator helps us to see not the opposition between authenticity and false covers but the active negotiation between the experience of subjectivity and acts of social performance. Almost every single personal account in this poignant book suggests that authenticity is not an integral or a priori thing but a palimpsest of identifications, layered and ridden with internal contradictions. If anything, Yoshino demonstrates the psychoanalytic insight that we are every one of us the sum of the history of the ghosts of others whom we have taken in. When, for example, the narrator realizes that after years of Japanese school training, his sister "is no longer passing as Japanese, but that she was Japanese,"[6] he has located a highly imbricated dynamic between essence and performance, be-tween body and discipline. And when this same voice invites us to wit-ness the beauty of the "gold vest" that helped him to come out—the one that spoke of "jackdaw craving" and the one that "drove [his] invisible difference to the surface and held it there"[7]—how can we help but see the vital and profound place that fantasy occupies in the imaginary act of self-recognition? We are given the cover that uncovers. What allows the subject to emerge from the closet is not liberating nakedness but another costume—yet never "just" a costume. As Yoshino tells us, "it did become me, and . . . I could become it."[8]

The "subject" that emerges out of Baker's performances is indeed an eccentric one, one whose contours are limned by borrowed clad-ding and whose animation derives from objectivity. If what we deem to be immutable is in fact mutable and what we believe to be surface may be profoundly ontologically structuring, then we would need to rearticulate the very assumptions (authenticity, identity, shared uni-versal humanity, etc.) on which the rhetoric of freedom is built. The issue is less the distinction between immutable and mutable traits, or between essence and superficiality, and more about how these two sets of signifiers constitute each other. In the end, it is not a question of who is the fetishist and who is the fetishized but rather how both the colonial/racist imagination and its antidote share a predicament of embodiment. If anything, the history that we have been tracing shows us that it is the crisis of visuality, rather than the allocation of visibility, that constitutes one of the most profound challenges for American democratic recognition today.

In a sense, this book has been exploring different ways of understanding self-fashioning that do not have recourse to ideas of individualistic agency or of a naked self awaiting dress. Baker's life work seems to me to acknowledge the complicated and fraught dynamic between ontology and social representation; it also exemplifies the complex and diverse ways in which notions of "self" and "self-as-art" maintain a dynamic intimacy that is as ironic as it is promising. Her disappearance into appearance rewrites both the regressive and progressive histories that encode Black female skin. She is neither the willfully subversive agent whom critics hoped for nor the broken subject whom history demanded. Instead, turning her skin into cloth, she has claimed for herself the abject subject's right to weather (or wear) the crisis of subjectivity—that crisis being the volatile fluctuation between person and thingness, between body and husk. The "body" of Baker is both more and less than the thing that we thought it. And "it" leads us not to the separation of essence and appearance but to an animated relay between epidermal certitude and stylistic vicissitude in the making of racial legibility.

10

Back to the Museum

In 1933, Josephine Baker had her own chance to look back on modernism. When asked for her thoughts on modern art, she replied:

> I am so old-fashioned, so stupid maybe because I think that when one looks at a painting one has to be able to see right away what it is supposed to mean. . . . Take the other day, a rich woman . . . showed me with ostentatious enthusiasm a very small painting. She had paid an extraordinary amount, eh oh? Et ah! . . . [She asked me] whether I thought it was great. It was by him, you know, Pinazaro, or what is his name, the one everyone talks about?

"Picasso?" [the interviewer asks].

> Right, Picasso, and it was nothing but a few lines. They weren't even straight. You know, I find that terrible! Now, you can certainly say that I talk about things I don't understand. Well, let me respond to you then in telling you a fairy tale by Andersen: "Once upon a time there was a king who had a closet full of clothes, one more luxurious than the next . . ."[1]

One can take this comment as Baker's revenge, a jab at modernism as all appearance without substance, with her own art in contrast as all nakedness but full of essence. But our study of Baker has shown us that the visible is hardly a given and that the disparity between superficiality and substance can never be taken for granted. Baker's own performances insist upon and play relentlessly with the tension between what is readily seen and what is not, just as they exploit and invert the difference between worth and waste, art and counterfeit. If

Second Skin. Second edition. Anne Anlin Cheng, Oxford University Press. © Oxford University Press 2023.
DOI: 10.1093/oso/9780197748381.003.0010

civilized value reveals its empty foundation through its "ostentatious" willingness to pay for overpriced art, then Baker's coy response should remind us that her art, too, pivots on the ability to move between the invisible and the visible, between waste and gold.[2] Indeed, what could be more like the emperor in his new clothes than the stripper who does not strip or who, when she does, wears her nakedness like a splendid second skin?

For me, the story of Baker has been the story of how modern visuality comes to confront the miscegenation that gave it birth. The excluded colonial subject as well as the imperial subject participated in the modern dream of the second skin. More than gesturing to the ideological instability of colonial or modernist representations, Baker's career and its impact signal a new order of visuality. And that new order has everything to do with how the theatricalization of race breaks open rather than securing the borders of racial legibility. Baker in theater, film, photography, and architecture does not merely give us a visual object; rather, she teaches us how we see (as) modern subjects. Baker's iconography is most intriguing when it disrupts the conditions of its own visibility and is most vital when it (not exclusively tethered to personal intentionality) works to generate new terms of visibility.

The visual culture surrounding the racialized, female body, understood to be one of the most pernicious examples of masculinist, colonial imagination, tells stories not just of domination and shame but also of mutual desires, defenses, productivities, and longings. The very nature of what constitutes "naked skin" becomes the dramatic and philosophical plane on which Baker's performances wrought their most visually arresting and confounding ideograms, challenging us to confront the fraught and ongoing dilemma of how to *see* raced bodies at the intersection of historic materiality and early-century semiotics. As with the Hans Christian Andersen parable (by the way, it was the first story Baker learned to recite in full in French), what is most interesting about Baker is neither the question of superficiality nor power's impenetrability but the conditions of the visible itself.

In the end, we see Baker's denial of Pablo Picasso not only as an arch imitation of the latter's much-publicized denial of his knowledge of African art but also as enacting a dexterous substitution. For, even as she dismisses the abstraction of modern art, her choice of

words perversely brings up the conceptual aspects of her own performative style (figure 10.1). That is to say, her words remind us of
the profound empathy between high modernist style and the restless
contour that *is* her art, itself a dynamic play on "a few lines that are
not even straight."

Fig. 10.1

Illustrations

Color Inserts:

Paul Colin, "Josephine Baker in Banana Skirt." © Artists Rights
Society (ARS), New York/ADAGP, Paris.

Elie Nadelman, "Man in Open Air." The Museum of Modern Art,
New York. Digital image © The Museum of Modern Art/
Licensed by SCALA/Art Resource, NY.

"Paris, France: May 1926. Josephine Baker (1906–1975),
Colorized photo. © Lipnitzki/Roger-Viollet/The
Image Works.

Josephine Baker with her leopard, Chiquita. Illustration by Jean
Rumeau, 1931. Courtesy of Jean-Claude Baker
Foundation, NY.

Notes

Chapter 1

1. See hooks, *Black Looks*, 61–79; Parks, "The Rear End Exists"; Sharpley-Whiting, *Black Venus*, 105–118.
2. Stuart, "Looking at Josephine Baker," 142.
3. This book is indebted to the insights of critics who have revealed the deep imbrications, if not downright identicalness, between "Modernism" and "Primitivism": Douglas, *Terrible Honesty*; Edwards, *The Practice of Diaspora*; Gilroy, *The Black Atlantic*; and Lemke, *Primitivist Modernism*. Lemke, for one, demonstrates that even as fantasies of black art were instrumental in forming white modernism, white European culture was also instrumental in shaping black artistic expressions, arguing that when it comes to racial fantasies, the boundaries of ownership and objecthood cannot be disciplined or controlled no matter how much ideology might wish them to be. The story of modernist primitivism is thus a tale about appropriation and reappropriation, about imagined origins and reimagined futures. At the same time, it is noticeable that even Lemke, who has written one of the most astute treatises on modernist primitivism that steps outside of binary terms, nonetheless falls back on a binaristic discourse when it comes to Baker, observing that "Josephine Baker appealed to colonialist fantasies of the exotic" (97) and that Baker "adapted the racist stereotypes by which black people had been oppressed and exploited them for her own commercial success" (103).
4. Pierre de Régnier, review for *Candide* (November 25, 1925), quoted in Sauvage, *Les mémoires de Joséphine Baker*, 11–12. Also quoted without documentation by Baker and Chase, *Josephine Baker*, 5; Rose, *Jazz Cleopatra*, 19; Haney, *Naked at the Feast*, 20. Nancy Cunard also registers similar confusions about Baker's race and gender in her contribution to her edited *Negro* anthology: "is it a youth, is it a girl? . . . she seems to whiten as we gaze at her" (329).
5. Cummings, "Vive la Folie!" 20.

6. When Virginia Woolf made her famously unequivocal claim that "on or about December, 1910, human character changed," she tied this sea change directly to Roger Fry's influential exhibition "Manet and the Post-Impressionists" of the same year. This exhibition not only introduced French avant-garde art to England some thirty years after its initial appearance in France but also established "primitive objects" as foundational tropes for Modernist aesthetic theories. That exhibition, along with Fry's essays "The Art of the Bushman" (1910) and "Negro Sculpture" (1920), made primitive objects the occasion for an emerging modern aesthetic. For an account of this history, see Torgovnick, *Gone Primitive*, 85–104. For the quote from Woolf, see Woolf, "Mr. Bennett and Mrs. Brown," 388.

7. Glover, "Postmodern Homegirl." See also Stovall, *Paris Noir* for a definitive study of the cosmopolitan community of black American expatriate writers, artists, musicians, and intellectuals in Paris from 1914 to the present. Jules-Rosette's *Black Paris* offers another important study of African writers in Paris, from the early Negritude movement to the mid-1990s. The Parisian cabaret clientele facing Baker were therefore hardly strangers to so-called exotic imports. Baker's debut itself also saw seasoned viewers such as the poet E. E. Cummings, the filmmaker Jean Cocteau, the painter Fernand Léger, and the American expatriate New Yorker writer Janet Flanner.

8. Although there is no existing monograph on Baker's art as a serious engagement with modernist aesthetics, there is a group of key essays that have treated Baker's art with critical patience to which this book is indebted. I am thinking of Coffman, "Uncanny Performances in Colonial Narratives"; Henderson, "Josephine Baker and La Revue Nègre"; Ngai, "Black Venus, Blonde Venus"; and Scheper, " 'Of La Baker, I Am a Disciple.' " Jules-Rosette's exceptional biography of Baker, *Josephine Baker in Art and Life*, also provided much-needed resources. This critical biography is especially instructive in its keen attention to the constructed nature of Baker's self-representation. Finally, as I was completing this book, Brown's study *Babylon Girls* was published. Although I would argue that Baker exceeds the assessment offered by Brown that she was finally a symptom of "the masculinist European fantasies of the female colonial subject imported to the city" (251), I found Brown's study to be extremely helpful in providing contexts for understanding Baker in relation to the larger history of early modern black female performers.

9. Fanon, *Black Skin, White Masks*, 112; Doane, *Femmes Fatales*, 223; Bhabha, *The Location of Culture*, 78.

10. I am thinking, for example, of Freud's work on hysteria and the case of Dora and how his development of the concepts of trauma and psychical reality struggled with the impulse to posit a "real" rather than "imagined" scene of seduction. The psychoanalysts Jean Laplanche and J. B. Pontalis point out rather shrewdly that the moment Freud discovers "psychical reality" is also the moment he submits it to the law of the real. That is, the psyche is freed only to be irrevocably tethered to the biological. See Freud, "Fragment of an Analysis of a Case of Hysteria" (1905/1901), *SE* 7:3; Laplanche and Pontalis, "Fantasy and the Origins of Sexuality."

11. Woolf, "Modern Fiction"; Wilde, *The Picture of Dorian Grey*; Warhol in a 1966 interview with the *East Village Other*, in Goldsmith, Kostenbaum, and Wolf, *I'll Be Your Mirror*, 85; Kenner, *The Mechanic Muse*.

12. Freud, "The Ego and the Id" (1923), *SE* 19:19; Laplanche, *Life and Death in Psychoanalysis*, 81. For a thought-provoking treatment of Freud's "archaeology metaphor," see Altman, "Freud among the Ruins."

13. In recent years, with the advent of new materials and digital technologies, the lure of the surface has drawn architectural theorists and practitioners alike to explore concepts such as "sentient," "performative," or "intelligent" surfaces. The "Skin Show" at the Cooper Hewitt National Design Museum (2002), organized by Ellen Lupton, and Toshiko Mori's "Immaterial/Ultramaterial" exhibition at Material Connexion (2002) attest to the millennial attraction of developments in material science and fabrication technology and underscore broader interests in the fraught relations among bodies, structures, and appearances. Recently, the Cooper Hewitt hosted a sequel to its "Skin Show," which presented examples of new products, furniture, fashion, architecture, and media that are expanding the limits of the outer surface. Reflecting the convergence of natural and artificial life, this exhibition highlighted how enhanced and simulated skins appear throughout the contemporary environment.

14. For the larger history of the role of racial difference in the philosophic making of the European Enlightenment, see Eze, *Race and the Enlightenment*. For a more specific history about the role of skin collecting in British Victorian culture, see Sigel, *Governing Pleasures*, especially the chapter on "Sexuality Raw and Cooked," 50–80. For an intriguing look at British museum culture and morbidity, see Daly, "That Obscure Object of Desire."

15. In *Reading in Detail*, Schor addresses the feminization and rejection of the ornamental detail on the modern surface in the making of aesthetic idealism. Indeed, she names Adolf Loos, whom we will meet in this study, as a

prime example of the modern philosophic rejection of the feminized ornamental detail. In *White Walls, Designer Dresses*, Wigley highlights the critical and fraught conversation with femininity in the history of the making of the modern white wall. I build on these scholars' insights to suggest that race, too, has written its indelible traces on those modern surfaces. The history of idealist aesthetics, exemplified by the nonornamental, clean, white surface, is a history not only of sexual difference, as Schor and Wigley so beautifully demonstrate, but also of racial difference. It is also, I believe, a history that foregrounds the failure, not the triumph, of these differences.

16. Fanon, *Black Skin, White Masks*, 112.
17. Fanon, *Black Skin, White Masks*, 109.

Chapter 2

1. *Action*, April 1920. Quoted by Lemke in *Primitivist Modernism*, 34–35.
2. This interview was conducted in 1937 but was not published until 1974, in Malraux's *La tête d'obsidienne* (English translation: *Picasso's Mask*, 1976). Also quoted by Lemke, *Primitivist Modernism*, 35.
3. This story of Picasso's encounter with African masks, often seen as a primal moment of modern art, is repeatedly told as an instance of colonial disgust and appropriation. Both Rosalind Krauss and Hal Foster have famously read this scene as a moment of colonial appropriation. (See Krauss, "Preying on 'Primitivism'"; Foster, "The Primitive Unconscious.") Rose, in *Jazz Cleopatra*, 42, used this story as the backdrop and analogy for the European reception of Baker. As Francette Pacteau points out regarding this same scene, "the association of the stench of decay with the image of black femininity, . . . in turn, in the painting [Les *Demoiselles d'Avignon*], is assimilated into a dangerous sexuality" (Pacteau, *The Symptom of* Beauty, 132). I want to suggest in what follows a different reading of and inflection in Picasso's "confession."
4. Gilot and Lake, *Life with Picasso*, 266. Also quoted by Lemke, *Primitivist Modernism*, 58.
5. Morrison, *The Bluest Eye*, 165.
6. William Rubin's *Primitivism in 20th Century Art* is, of course, a foundational text for outlining the long history of "African importation" into modern art. Rubin reads this scene of pivotal encounter in the museum as a scene of projection; that is, Picasso projects his maternal anxieties onto the tribal objects he sees. I am suggesting here that the anxieties are not

only personal but also racial and cultural and that the objects are working on and through their viewer as well.

Chapter 3

1. Loos, *Spoken into the Void*, 66–67. Considered one of the first innovators of modernist architectural style, Loos was born in or around 1870, a contemporary of Charles Rennie Mackintosh, Frank Lloyd Wright, and Auguste Perret. Le Corbusier and Ludwig Mies van der Rohe would come half a generation later.

2. For Semper, the first canvas is the human skin, and the first architectural space is the open pen, made of woven skins and other organic materials: "[I]t remains certain *that the beginning of building coincides with the beginning of textile.* . . . We might recognize the *pen*, bound together from sticks and branches, and the interwoven *fence* as the earliest vertical spatial structure that man *invented.* . . . For it remains certain that the use of the crude weaving that started with the pen—as a means to make the 'home,' the *inner* separated from the *outer life*, and as the formal creation of the idea of space—undoubtedly preceded the wall, even the most primitive one constructed out of stone or any other material" (Semper, *The Four Elements of Architecture*, 254). Wolfgang Herrmann presents some further translations of previously undiscovered texts by Semper, such as the following on the importance of the hearth: "Before men thought of erecting tents . . . they gathered around the open flame. . . . The hearth is the germ, the embryo, of all social institutions . . . the hearth became a place of worship. . . . It was a moral symbol. . . . The house altar was the first object to be singled out for adornment" (Herrmann, *Gottfried Semper*, 198). For more on the relationship between Loos and Semper, see Rykwert, "Adolf Loos."

3. Loos, "Ornament and Crime," 100.

4. Loos, "Ornament and Crime," 101.

5. The purifying "Law of Ripolin," named after an opaque white coat of paint favored by Le Corbusier, alludes to the imperative coat of whitewash that Le Corbusier believed would make people "masters of themselves" by cleansing the home of sentimental kitsch and the "accretions of dead things from the past." See Le Corbusier, *The Decorative Art of Today*, 185–192. See also Wigley, *White Walls, Designer Dresses*, for an insightful treatise on Le Corbusier's relationship to color and the gender politics therein.

Following Wigley's remarks, it is difficult not to see also in Le Corbusier's aesthetic and theoretical trajectory toward the "whitewash" a parable for his less noted relation to racial difference. Le Corbusier's rejection of colors in favor of an impassive whiteness itself partakes of a trajectory in his own work where he moves from an early fascination with so-called exotic and primitive colors (exemplified by his *Le voyage d'orient/Journey to the East*, originally written in 1911 and partially published in French in 1966) to what appears to be a renunciation of that preference in the Law of Ripolin. I will suggest later on that Le Corbusier's aesthetic development is intimately linked to his complex views about racial difference.

6. See Freud, "Group Psychology and the Analysis of the Ego" (1921), *SE*, 18:72; see also Freud, "Civilization and Its Discontents" (1930/1929), *SE*, 21:5–246. While there is no direct evidence that Loos read Freud, there is still much to suggest that Loos was acquainted with Freud's work. Freud was quite visible in the print media beginning soon after the publication of "The Interpretation of Dreams" (1899/1900, *SE*, 4). See Tichy and Zwettler-Otte, *Freud in der Presse*. Freud and Loos also shared common friends, and both published in the *Neue Freie Presse*, the *New York Times* of its era and place. Loos would also have seen favorable mention of Freud in Karl Kraus's journal *Die Fackel*, where a review of "Three Essays on Sexuality" (1905), *SE*, 7:125, appeared. Finally, I thank Leo Lensing for sharing his knowledge of Vienna at the turn of the century and for pointing the way to further research on the social world in which Freud and Loos circulated.

7. Quetglas, "Lo placentero," 2. Quetglas's commentary on Loos was translated and quoted in Colomina's foundational essay "The Split Wall," 92.

8. Colquhoun, *Modern Architecture*, 82–83.

9. Simmel, "The Metropolis and Mental Life." We will return to Simmel later because, in fact, Simmel's idea of an anonymous surface is designed not to erase but to accentuate the modern man's personality. Hence, in Simmel, we once again see the paradox of the anonymous surface as denudement and ornamentation.

10. Quetglas, "Lo Placentero," 2. Quoted and translated by Colomina, "The Split Wall," 92.

11. Although Loos was antiornament, he was not anticraft per se. On the contrary, he deeply valued what he considered genuine craftsmanship. For him, ornament connotes the waste of human labor, money, and material, while genuine craft is still to be celebrated. See, for example, his meditations in essays such as "Glass and Clay," "Footwear," or "Shoemakers," all collected in his *Spoken into the Void*. Both Joseph Rykwert and Hal Foster

have commented on Loos's insistent separation on the difference between utility and craft. See Rykwert, "Adolf Loos"; Foster, *Prosthetic Gods*, especially 75–87.

12. Colomina, "The Split Wall"; Colomina, *Privacy and Publicity*.

13. Adolf Loos, shorthand record of a conversation in Pilsen, 1930. Documented in the Adolf Loos Study Center, City of Prague Museum, exhibition of the floor plans for the Müllers' villa.

14. Anzieu, *The Skin Ego*, 40.

15. For an extended reading of Anzieu, see Pacteau, *The Symptom of Beauty*, 152–156.

16. Anzieu, *The Skin Ego*, 40.

17. Colquhoun, *Modern Architecture*, 81.

18. Colquhoun, *Modern Architecture*, 82

19. Colquhoun, *Modern Architecture*, 81.

20. Colquhoun, *Modern Architecture*, 82.

21. See Doane, *Femmes Fatales*; Walton, *Fair Sex, Savage Dreams*; Khanna, *Dark Continents*; and Seshadri-Crooks, *Desiring Whiteness*.

22. Most cultural historians agree that, fueled by medical and scientific advancements, a shift occurred in the perception of the human skin in the eighteenth and nineteenth centuries where what was once seen as porous in medieval times gradually became seen as bounded (that is, something that provides bodily limitation and enables individuation and self-becoming). See Benthien, *Skin*; Connor, *The Book of Skin*; and Fend, "Bodily and Pictorial Surfaces." My point here is that the " 'closed neuronal organism' of modernity" (Fend, "Bodily and Pictorial Surfaces," 312) is in fact quite *fragile*. Alongside this growing view of skin as impenetrable wall of separation in the nineteenth century is a profound anxiety about the singularity of skin, an anxiety that I suggest is not unreflected by the development of racial history in the modern world.

Chapter 4

1. There is much more work yet to be done on Baker's influence on and affinities with other modern burlesque stars, such as Gypsy Rose Lee, whose act was also often about stripping to reveal more cloth/fabric/ornament underneath. One can also relate Baker's art to other figures such as Mata Hari, Loie Fuller, and Clara Bow, all of whom share a remarkable reliance on fabric and sartorial manipulation. For a study of Fuller in

particular and her architectural deployment of cloth, see Garelick, *Electric Salome*.

2. Bentley, *Sisters of Salome*; Clifton, Ainslie, and Cook, *Baby Oil and Ice*; Shteir, *Striptease*; Wortley, *A Pictorial History of Striptease*; Wallace and Wallechinsky, *The People's Almanac*.

3. By the "zoological" I refer to the ways in which theatrical spaces such as the Moulin Rouge and the Folies Bergère would draw their modes of dramatic presentation and mise en scène from venues such as the Jardin Zoologique d'Acclimatation in Paris at the turn of the century, where the racialized and colonial subject (from the Arabic "snake charmer" to the "Venus Hottentot") would be displayed not only caged like savage beasts but also often surrounded by animals. See Blanchard, Deroo, and Manceron, *Le Paris noir*; Stovall, *Paris Noir*.

4. Biographical evidence, especially from the latter half of Baker's life, is often invoked as testimony to her progressive politics, mostly in an effort to ward off or refute the political embarrassment posed by her early theatrical work. Biographers, critics, and reviewers alike cite her work in the French Resistance during World War II, her participation in the American civil rights movement, her self-named "Rainbow Tribe" of adopted children, and her dream of creating a utopian, multicultural society. But as Jayna Brown points out, Baker's alliance with France also operated to "obscure real colonial relations" (Brown, *Babylon Girls*, 261). I would add that Baker complicates the so-called real colonial relations in other ways as well. This is why the paradigm of attributing all or no agency to Baker (not to mention conflating biography with subjectivity) is inadequate to address the dynamic exchanges provoked by her performances between theatrics and spectatorship, between performance and the performer, and between cultural practice and social imagination. The liberal gesture (for both Baker and most of us today) is not free from imperialist desires. The "Rainbow Tribe," for instance, as a "collection" of children of different races teeters uneasily between a bold dream of diversity and a disquieting repetition of imperial desire. Her self-fashioning as the Black Madonna/Marianna, as biographer Jules-Bennett so well documents, for another example, underscores the uneasy affinity between recuperation and exoticization. Indeed, we see this disturbance with uncomfortable clarity when we turn to a semibiographical children's book that Baker wrote, titled *The Rainbow Children* (1958), which tells the story of a one-eyed little black duck who ran away from home after suffering exclusion and abuse among her kin. The black duck wanders all over the world to one day find refuge in a beautiful garden filled with children of all colors

and races who teach the duck how to love herself. The children in the story are named after Baker's real-life adopted children, and they are under the care of "Marianna," who does not appear until the last pages of the book. The reader might expect to see a drawing rendition of Baker herself given the biographical nature of the fairy tale. Yet instead of Baker or a Baker-like figure, we get a blond, blue-eyed goddess figure. The point here is not to decry Baker's racial politics but to underscore how power tends to reproduce itself, even for and within the subject whom it has injured.

5. Karen Dalton and Henry Louis Gates Jr., for instance, memorialize her for embodying "the energy of jazz" and the "elegance of the Black Venus" (Dalton and Gates, "Josephine Baker and Paul Colin," 910). Michael Borshuk offers an example of the subversion reading: "[Baker] was able to diminish the negative power of governing stereotypes . . . by situating herself at the exaggerated limits of those distorted representations . . . thus revealing the illegitimacy of white concocted notions of Negro Primitivism and eroticism by situating them within the self-conscious illusory spectacle of the stage" (Borshuk, "An Intelligence of the Body," 50). As appealing as Borshuk's reading of Baker is for those of us trying to understand our fascination with her, the truth is that it is very difficult to imagine her audience as having been shocked into a self-conscious recognition of their own "concocted notions"; they were most likely enjoying the spectacle too much. The problem with this kind of redemptive interpretation act is that it can forget the fact that subversion always tends to reproduce the very stereotypes it means to dismantle in the first place. As Judith Butler has pointed out, subversion has its limitations (Butler, *Bodies That Matter*).

6. Primitivism and Orientalism have produced a rhetoric about the racial other that is characterized by ambivalence: the language of idealization going hand in hand, for instance, with the language of denigration. This negative capability converges most notably in the figure of the racialized woman, who came to embody the epitome of both sexual vitality and moral decay. Historian Sander Gilman's seminal work on Saartjie Baartman, also known as the Venus Hottentot, for example, perfectly documents this conjunction (Gilman, *Difference and Pathology*).

7. For Mae Henderson, Baker cultivates modernist references and technologies as much as she caters to European notions of the primitive. For Sianne Ngai, Baker instantiates the practice of imitation that forms the foundation of a particularly Modernist representational strategy. For Jeanne Scheper, it is Baker's ability to cannibalize multiple identities that renders her such a seductive sign of resignification for contemporary artists working from transnational, black diasporic, black feminist, and

queer perspectives. These efforts to reexamine Baker's style and its legacy suggest the need to explore further the particularity and implications of Baker's problematic relationship to notions of imitation and agency. See Henderson, "Josephine Baker and La Revue Nègre"; Ngai, "Black Venus, Blonde Venus"; Scheper, "'Of La Baker.'"

8. Baker first wore the banana skirt in 1926 in the dance "Fatou" during her show *La folie du jour*. It immediately became one of her trademarks. The character that Baker played, Fatou, is named after a character in Pierre Loti's novel *The Marriage of Loti*, a colonial fantasy about a European man's romance with a "native" woman. So Baker was performing a character that was already an existing citation about the European fantasy of savage femininity.

9. Mullen, *Trimmings*, 47.

10. Although Baker's banana skirt did vary over time in terms of material and stylization, it is revealing how critics and journalists tended to treat the physical appearance of the bananas as stable and then invariably attribute either a reputed softness or hardness to them. Ylza Habel alludes to Baker's "perky bananas" (Habel, "To Stockholm with Love"); Phyllis Rose describes the bananas as "perky, good natured phalluses" (Rose, *Jazz Cleopatra*, 97); Marjorie B. Garber calls them "tusks" (Garber, *Vested Interests*, 279); and Susan Robinson attributes a brittle hardness to those bananas, calling them "lacquered" and "ceramic" (Robinson, "Josephine Baker"). On the other side of the perky bananas, we find Dalton and Gates, who describe the costume as "a girdle of drooping bananas" and "flaccid phalluses" (Dalton and Gates, "Josephine Baker and Paul Colin," 917). Philip M. Ward entertains both possibilities: "[Baker's] bananas bounced and bobbed like so many flaccid (but perhaps, in the imagination of her audience, tumescent) phalluses" (Ward, "The Electric Body").

11. France and Britain were among the first European countries to import bananas on a large scale beginning in the early 1920s. See Welch, *Survival by Association*, for an account of this history. Debates over whether Antillean bananas were really French as part of the ongoing struggle over market rights and protection throughout the twentieth century reflect the enduring pressure of European imperial interests in that region. For a history of the banana plantations in the Americas and Carribean, see Moberg et al., *Banana Wars*; Chapman, *Bananas!*: Koeppel, *Banana*. For an intriguing account of the US's involvement in the "banana wars," see Goffe, *When Banana Was King*. I am also indebted to Felicia McCarren's wonderful essay on Baker's bananas as symbolic of the capital of commodity (McCarren, "The Use-Value of 'Josephine Baker'").

12. Freud, "Fetishism" (1927), *SE*, 21:149.

13. See Bhabha, *The Location of Culture*, 66–84. For Bhabha, it is the entwined nature of projection and compensation that psychically fuels skewed racial perceptions. Consequently, the stereotype—or the racial fetish—enables the production of an identity that is predicated as much on mastery and pleasure as it is on anxiety and difference, for it is a form of multiple and contradictory belief in its recognition of difference and the disavowal of it. In foregrounding the anxiety haunting the apparent gestures of mastery and certitude behind every production and assertion of the stereotype, Bhabha is able to build an extensive critique of colonial authorial integrity.

14. For a wonderful dramatization and unpacking of the banana complications that I am detailing here, see the animated film *Les Triplettes de Belleville* (directed by Sylvain Chomet, France/Belgium/Canada/UK, 2003), in which a metadiegetic cartoon incarnation of Baker makes a guest appearance doing the banana-belt dance. In this rendition, Baker's banana skirt comes undone in a moment of striptease exposure. The French men in the diegetic audience rush the stage in a frenzy, exposing the white male desire that, to borrow Scheper's words, "is the drive for natural resources imagined as a drive for the female body" (Scheper, "'Of La Baker,'" 79). The object of desire in this scene is *not* the naked woman but the naked *bananas*. For even as the viewer expects the diegetic audience to ravish the now-naked Baker huddling onstage, they instead chase after the scattered bananas like monkeys themselves. The scene thus dramatizes not the drive for the female body—that body is left to the side of the stage as the scene progresses—but the drive for the bananas, thereby unleashing a homoerotic potential as well as a Primitivist identification, even as it grants Baker a parodic phallus. The multiple options here underscore the racially and sexually multivalent and ambiguous symbolic registers encompassed by the conceit of the banana.

15. Hence we get the ambivalent figure of the Medusa, after whom Freud names one of his three seminal essays on fetishism. Freud identifies this famously beautiful woman whose hair turned into a nest of snakes as the very symbol of femininity as fetish in his essay "Medusa's Head" (1922/1940, *SE*, 18:273). But are we supposed to see Medusa's cut-off head as a symbol of feminine castration or her hissing snakes as her threatening phallic power? The answer is both, and it is a paradox that only makes sense when we understand that the fetish is designed not, as many thought, to erase difference but in fact to maintain and organize that difference into what the poet John Keats calls "negative capability": the ability to entertain

two radically opposing thoughts at the same time. So the fetish is as confessional as it is disavowing.

16. As I have argued elsewhere, our society needs to develop a more nuanced approach to recognition of racial injury where we try to understand that wound as deeply structuring without having to naturalize it. I have been drawn to the concept of racial melancholia because it recognizes the fundamental instability between subject and object, between performance and essence. I see this Baker project as extending and exploring the implications raised by that earlier book: the challenges of reading a subject both too visible and hidden; the vexed problem of locating agency in the face of compromised desires; the critical need to understand the possibilities of what I had called an "ethics of immersion" (Cheng, *The Melancholy of Race*, 188). In a sense, *Second Skin* is about the challenges of understating that ethics of immersion at the level of critical practice: what kind of hermeneutics is called for in the face of contaminated pleasure?

Chapter 5

1. A copy of the plans for the Baker House can be found in the Adolf Loos Archive in the Albertina Museum, Vienna. Accounts of the Baker-Loos relationship are vague and mostly secondhand. Baker herself curiously never mentions Loos or this design in her memoirs or letters. Detailed accounts of the design itself and the Loos-Baker connection come secondhand from Loos's student and collaborator Kurt Unger (in a letter to Ludwig Münz on July 23, 1935, in Münz and Künstler, *Adolf Loos*, 195). Also cited by Groenendijk and Vollaard, *Adolf Loos*, 32.

2. Loos, "Ornament and Crime," 187.

3. Groenendijk and Vollaard, *Adolf Loos*, 34.

4. See Kurt Ungers, Loos's collaborator on the Baker project, in a letter to Ludwig Münz, in Münz and Künstler, *Adolf Loos*, 195.

5. Quetglas, "Lo placentero," 2.

6. Colomina, "The Split Wall"; el-Dahdah, "The Josephine Baker House" (including a digital, sequential reconstruction of the Baker House by Stephen Atkinson); Tanzer, "Baker's Loos"; Berman, "Civilized Planes"; Davis, "Signifyin' Josephine"; Henderson, "Bachelor Culture."

7. Groenendijk and Vollaard labeled the Baker House as "prurient setting" (*Adolf Loos*, 32).

8. Colomina, "The Split Wall," 75n4.

9. Colomina, "The Split Wall," 90.
10. Here we might think of Philip Johnson's Glass House (New Canaan, CT, completed in 1984), where its famed transparent walls also effect a curious opacity in its reflective quality.
11. Baker often appeared topless in Parisian and other European theatrical venues, though she is often clothed, albeit scantily, in photographs in anticipation of international audiences. Thus, for instance, although she performed the bananas-belt dance topless, she is photographed with breastplates in deference to the more puritanical tastes of American audiences.
12. Wilde, *The Picture of Dorian Grey*, 41.
13. The film's final disavowal—when the entire plot gets erased and shown to be all a daydream—serves as a last-ditch and not very persuasive effort to protect the master/Max from this revelation. This fantasy of denial, by the way, embodies its own visual avowals, since the film ends with Max's now complete "book of civilization" being scattered to the winds.
14. Leader, *Stealing the Mona Lisa*, 32.
15. Rose, *Jazz Cleopatra*, XXX.
16. Brown, *Babylon Girls*, XXX; Haney, *Naked at the Feast*, XXX; Jules-Rosette, *Josephine Baker*, XXX; Rose, *Jazz Cleopatra*, XXX.
17. For a wonderfully detailed account of Baker's residences as part of her elaborate public-self making, see Jules-Rosette, *Josephine Baker*, especially 13–46.
18. Diane Davis describes the skin of the Baker House as "fetishized" (Davis, "Signifyin' Josephine," 34). Farès el-Dahdah describes Loos as the fetishist and interprets the "daubing" on the surface of the Baker House as a direct reference to Loos's writings on tattoos (el-Dahdah, "The Josephine Baker House," 77). Susan R. Henderson labels that surface as "'tattooed' striations" that "express the tribal roots of its patroness" (Henderson, "Bachelor Culture," 131). Elana Shapira likewise links that facade to Loos's ideas on criminality and tattoos (Shapira, "Dressing a Celebrity," 6). Finally, Ila Berman also references this connection between the Baker House facade and tattoos, although he, as we will see, finds this designation more problematic than accurate (Berman, "Civilized Planes").
19. Münz and Künstler, *Adolf Loos*, 195; Rykwert, "Adolf Loos," 72; Tournikiotis, *Adolf Loos*, 95. These critics describe the project as "African" without specifying what they mean by that assignation. What is clear is that they reflexively associate the house's exoticness to its proposed client. Contemporary criticism of the Baker House continues this assumption, though inflected with a clear postcolonial sensibility: see Burns, "A House

for Josephine Baker," as well as Colomina, "The Split Wall." For both, the house's design reveals its designer's racial and gender discriminations. Finally, the Baker House has also been associated with Orientalism, another strand of colonial projection. Kim Tanzer argues that the Baker House shares structural and design similarity to Loos's 1925 (also unbuilt) design for the Tientsin Exhibition Hall in northern China (Tanzer, "Baker's Loos").

20. This continuity of black-and-white design in Loos's body of works has also been observed by Shapira ("Dressing a Celebrity," 10–13).

21. For more on the history of Moorish design, see Fletcher, *Moorish Spain*; Barrucand and Bednorz, *Moorish Architecture in Andalusia*; Knowles, *Miller's 100 Years of the Decorative Arts*.

22. Loos, "Ornament and Crime," 100.

23. Loos, "Ornament and Crime," 100. Loos adds the erotic artist to the equation that connects racial degeneracy to criminality. According to Loos, whereas the primitive man cannot help but be an erotic artist, the modern man should know better. As Hal Foster observes, Loos is not just an antiornamentalist; he offers his dictum as a form of social critique (Foster, *Prosthetic Gods*). It is, in fact, a critique of art itself. But this rather Marxist critique is also elitist, because it is deeply linked to a racialized notion of temporal progress and development. Also see Schor, *Reading in Detail*; Wigley, *White Walls, Designer Dresses*. We will return to Foster's essay in more detail later.

24. Lombroso, *Criminal Man*, xxv. Allan Sekula points out that during the 1890s in particular, "a profusion of texts appeared in France and Italy offering photographic evidence of basic criminal types. Photographs and technical illustrations were deployed, not only against the body of the representative criminal, but also against the body as bearer and producer of its own, inferior representations. . . . For Lombroso, tattooing was a particular mark of atavism, since criminals shared the practice with presumably less evolved tribal peoples" (Sekula, "The Body and the Archive," 40).

25. Striped prison uniforms commonly used in the nineteenth century were abolished in the United States in the twentieth century precisely because their continued use as a badge of shame was considered undesirable and inhumane. See Pratt, *Punishment and Civilization*, 76.

26. An example of a "banana republic" would be Honduras, where the United Fruit, the Standard Fruit, and Sam Zemurray's Cuyamel Fruit companies dominated the country's key banana export sector and support sectors such as railways. The United Fruit Company was nicknamed "The Octopus" (El Pulpo) for its willingness to involve itself in politics, sometimes violently.

In 1910, Zemurray hired a group of armed men from New Orleans to stage a coup in Honduras to obtain beneficial treatment from the new government. Twenty-two years later, Zemurray would take over United Fruit in a hostile bid. Four decades after the 1910 coup, the directors of United Fruit played a role in convincing the Truman and Eisenhower administrations that the government of Colonel Jacobo Árbenz in Guatemala was secretly pro-Soviet, thus contributing to the CIA's decision to assist in overthrowing Árbenz's government in 1954. Pablo Neruda would denounce the dominance of foreign-owned banana producers in the politics of several Latin American countries in his poem "La United Fruit Co." That the Banana Republic that is a household name these days, that is, one of America's most staple retail chains ubiquitously found in almost all malls across the country, should be named after this violent history is more than ironic and bespeaks a specific historic and philosophic development. Some readers will undoubtedly recall the shift in the store's clothing line in the late '80s, when the original colonial nostalgia of the store became less politically palatable and less popular, and the company revamped itself and turned into the successful retail chain that it is today by pioneering the concept of an upscale but affordable, androgynous, and uniform style that champions the desirability and elegance of mass-reproduced clothes. Suddenly, fashion turns from the fetishization of the unique to the fetishization of the ordinary, producing that oxymoronic idea of a signature style that boasts of no signature. Not only should we recall Loos's foundational essay "Ornament and Crime," but we should also note that in light of the history that we are tracing here, the move toward democratization denotes neither a denial nor a correction but embodies in fact an evolution of imperial history. For colonial nostalgia has retailored itself as the form of a new mass-produced and mass-available sensibility: a new imperialism.

27. I am here suggesting that the notions of the female and the animal should be added to what Mark Seltzer has called the "body machine" (Seltzer, *Bodies and Machines*).

28. Loos, *Spoken into the Void*, 103.

29. Loos, *Spoken into the Void*, 102.

30. See, for example, Shapira, "Dressing a Celebrity," 9. That essay gestures to the complications of racial and gender discrimination in the Loos and Baker connection but tends to resort to traditionally gendered and class-based assumptions when it comes to revaluing Baker herself. For instance, Shapira sees this particular photo of Baker as subversive in that it offers a sign of Baker's "ladylikeness" in contrast to her more supposedly "African" image.

Chapter 6

1. The speakeasy/nightclub is, of course, a space of urbanity and transgression. One of the attractions that El Morocco held for the glitterati of the '20s through the '40s was the publicity afforded by having their pictures taken by the supper club's official photographer, Jerome Zerbe, something of a forefather of what we now call the paparazzi. These pictures would then appear in newspapers the next day with the telltale backdrop of the club's design of blue zebra-striped banquettes and contrasting parquet floors designed by Vernon MacFarlane.

2. Simmel, "The Metropolis and Mental Life." As a side note, the blasé attitude, according to Simmel, is developed as a defense against Taylorized environments. We might say, ironically, that in this account, we have traded the deadening discipline of a Taylorized environment for the deadening discipline of psychical boredom.

3. The invention of the electric elevator and the metal skeleton changed the skylines by making it possible to build to unprecedented heights and increasing the financial profit of a given plot of land. Then the development of fireproofing techniques came to support the external walls and the floors on the steel frame and in doing so reduced the mass of the wall to what Alan Colquhoun provocatively calls "a thin cladding" (Colquhoun, *Modern Architecture*, 37). See also Jordy, "Masonry Block and Metal Skeleton."

4. Freud, "On Narcissism," *SE*, XIV (1914–1916), 89.

5. Here we might think of the terraced and jewel-like crown of the Chrysler Building, for instance, as a skyscraper that is simulating a woman's gown. Architect William Van Alen's original design for the Chrysler Building called for a decorative jewel-like glass crown. It also featured a base in which the showroom windows were tripled in height and topped by twelve stories with glass-wrapped corners, producing, in effect, that pailletted look. Although that design was deemed too expensive, the revised version with the terraced crown that we now know still retains that ornamental effect. Various architectural details and especially the building's gargoyles were modeled after Chrysler automobile products such as the hood ornaments of the Plymouth, but even what seems like a masculinist, even phallic, decorative detail can embody a feminine trace precisely by being a decoration. This skyscraper therefore exemplifies not only the machine age in the 1920s but also that machine age's nostalgia for the human and, even more intriguingly, to recall Naomi Schor's work on the gendered

history of the detail, for feminine detail/ornamentation. Ann Douglas has also observed the "womb-likeness" of the highly masculinized skyscraper in her chapter "Skyscrapers, Airplanes, and Airmindedness: 'The Necessary Angel'" (Douglas, *Terrible Honesty*, 434–461).

6. Bacon, *Le Corbusier in America*, xiii–xv.
7. The drawing for this project can be found on the cover of this book.
8. According to Aldo Rossi, it was Loos's work on the Chicago Tribune Tower Competition that allowed Loos to grasp the "essence of American architecture." See the introduction by Rossi in Loos, *Spoken into the Void*, x–xii.
9. Le Corbusier, *When the Cathedrals Were White*, 42.
10. Berman, *All That Is Solid*, 165–168.
11. Le Corbusier, *When the Cathedrals Were* White, 158–161.
12. For a detailed account of Le Corbusier's tour in America and the professional and personal relationships he forged during this visit, see Bacon, *Le Corbusier in America*.
13. Le Corbusier, excerpt from lecture delivered at the Museum of Modern Art, New York, October 25, 1935; quoted by Bacon, *Le Corbusier in America*, 159.
14. "French Visitor Here."
15. Berman, *All That Is Solid*, 168.
16. Berman, *All That Is Solid*, 166–169.
17. See, for example, Bacon, *Le Corbusier in America*, 224–225.
18. Le Corbusier, *Precisions*, 124.
19. Le Corbusier made intimate drawings of Baker such as a pencil drawing of her sleeping in bed. He also designed a ballet for her. See Bacon, *Le Corbusier in America*, 322n18, 378n88; Samuel, *Le Corbusier*, 17–18; letters from Le Corbusier to Josephine Baker, February 4, 1935, and January 2, 1936, collected at Fondation Le Corbusier, Paris.
20. Le Corbusier, *Precisions*, 87.
21. Le Corbusier, *Precisions*, 12.
22. Anzieu, *The Skin Ego*, 101.
23. For works on the psychoanalytic notion of the sonorous maternal voice, see Rosolato, "La voix," 81; Anzieu, "L'enveloppe sonore," 173; Doane, "The Voice in the Cinema"; Silverman, *The Acoustic Mirror*, 72–100 Finally, see also Slovoj Zizek on Doris Day's maternal voice in Alfred Hitchcock's *The Man Who Knew Too Much* (Zizek, *Enjoy Your Symptom*, 118). Zizek discusses how Day's voice—specifically, a resonant, maternal, and noisy voice—acts as the key to saving and "capturing" her character's abducted son by filling up halls and penetrating walls. (My thanks to Shane Vogel

for his encouragement to think about Baker's voice in the context of my argument.)

24. Baker and Chase, *Josephine Baker*, 202–209.

25. "Don't Touch My Tomatoes" was written for Baker in her 1959 comeback stage revue *Paris mes amours*, some twenty years after Billie Holiday's rendition of "Strange Fruit," a song that I believe Baker's song references. "Sonny Boy" is Baker's rendition of the song made famous by Al Jolson, who performed that number in blackface in his film *The Singing Fool* (directed by Lloyd Bacon, 1928). By covering this song, Baker inserts the fantasies of black female voice and black maternity into engagement with the white patriarchy, blackface, and Jewish masculinity.

26. Baker starred in *La créole*, an opera by Jacques Offenbach, in 1934.

27. Quoted in Colquoun, *Modern Architecture*, 146. Originally in a 1929 letter from Le Corbusier to Madame Meyer, in Le Corbusier, *Oeuvre Complét*, Vol. *1, XX*; also quoted in Eleb-Vidal, "Hotel Particuliére," 175.

28. Baker and Chase, *Josephine Baker*, 80–81.

29. Baker and Chase, *Josephine Baker*, 80–81.

Chapter 7

1. Quoted in McLeod, *Charlotte Perriand*, 30–31.

2. Flanner, *Paris Was Yesterday*, XX; both Levinson and Hanry-Jaunet are quoted in Abatino, *Josephine Baker*, 37.

3. Rubin, *Primitivism in 20th Century Art*, 241–344.

4. Rubin, *Primitivism in 20th Century Art*, 17.

5. Rubin, *Primitivism in 20th Century Art*, 252.

6. Krauss, "Preying on 'Primitivism,' " 59.

7. Krauss, "Preying on 'Primitivism,' " 60; my emphasis.

8. Jules-Rosette, *Josephine Baker*, 137–142.

9. Jules-Rosette, *Josephine Baker*, 140.

10. Dyer, *White*; see especially 82–144. See also Dyer's discussion of lighting in *Heavenly Bodies*, 19–66.

11. Dyer, *White*, 78.

12. Barthes, *Mythologies*, 56–57.

13. Brown, *Glamour in Six Dimensions*, 145.

14. Meikle, *American Plastic*, 1. Barthes has also observed this connection between the *material nova* and early-century sensibilities. See Barthes, *Mythologies*, 97–99.

15. Wood, "Introduction," 4.

16. See Gaines, "Costume and Narrative," 205, for an interesting discussion of fabrics in classic Hollywood costumes that aim to simulate skin.

17. Shine has a long history of being associated with objectness and commodity. John Berger argues that the material rendering of the material world in oil is related to capital and exchange in sixteenth-century Europe, Hal Foster links the production of shine in Dutch paintings to commodity production, and Krista Thompson reminds us that shine has long served to signal black skin's commodification in the European imaginary. Here I want to suggest that Baker-shine, refracted through the contexts of Hollywood lighting, industrial revolution, and sculptural practices in the interwar years, offers a different *glanz* at Black skin. See Berger, *Ways of Seeing*; Foster, "The Art of Fetishism"; Thompson, "The Sound of Light."

18. Agamben, *Homo Sacre*, 6.

19. Brown, *A Sense of Things*, 137.

20. Brown, *A Sense of Things*, 138.

21. Jeffrey Meikle points out that the early uses of plastics were aimed to duplicate organic materials such as ivory and tortoise shell (Meikle, *American Plastics*, 10–14).

22. Thomas Hardy, *Tess of the d'Urvervilles* (New York: Penguin, 2003), 25.

23. In the genre of studio photography, the cult of the subject is paradoxically personlessness. The photograph is taken by a sleight of hand, unnoticed by the distracted sitter. Madame d'Ora, the Viennese photographer of Baker, for instance, sees staging as the true persona behind these images: "[The photographer] criticizes [the clients'] dress, decides a picture is to be taken of the hair or the hat, draped veils, lace and fur-coats . . . removes [their] jewellery, adorns them . . . and involves them in a conversation that will be stimulating and interesting. Then, suddenly, comes the announcement that the photograph is done. . . . The signals which the artist and the technical operator have exchanged have not been noticed by today's 'beauties.'" This is not to say that Baker has no agency whatsoever in these sittings, but it is to remind us not to conflate representation with self-representation and self-representation with agency. As Monika Faber, curator of the Madame D'Ora photography exhibition at Vassar College in 1987, observes, Madame D'Ora's "lighting management" "served more to create a photographic surface than characterize the person." In short, these photographs promise subjectivity or personality through, so to speak, cladding. See Faber, *D'Ora*, 11, 13.

24. Seltzer, *Bodies and Machines*, 140.

25. Spillers, "Mama's Baby, Papa's Maybe," 60.

26. Spillers, "Mama's Baby, Papa's Maybe," 61.

27. Spillers, "Mama's Baby, Papa's Maybe," 61.

28. This reading helps us understand, for instance, that memorable scene from the film *Zouzou*, when Zouzou/Baker's talent is discovered while she is dancing next to a larger-than-life shadow of herself, as another moment in which being-for-the-other may be seen as potentially coexisting with being-for-the-self, complicating the easy politics of specularity and performance that such a scene might normally suggest. Indeed, the entire film offers an extended meditation on the nature of doubleness: from her "twin brother" to the doubleness of Zouzou herself (inscribed even in her name).

29. Seltzer, *Bodies and Machines*, 13.

30. Kracauer writes of the British Tiller Girls: "When they formed an undulating snake, they radiantly illustrated the virtues of the conveyor belt; when they tapped their feet in fast tempo, it sounded like *business, business, business*; when they kicked their legs high with mathematical precision, they joyously affirmed the progress of rationalization; and when they kept repeating the same movements without interrupting their routine, one envisioned an uninterrupted chain of motor cars gliding in from the factories into the world" ("Girls and Crisis," 565). Kracauer, a student of Georg Simmel, is well known for his contention that the suppression of ornament in architecture has been displaced on or compensated by the ornament of the masses themselves. This ornamentation, however, supposedly does not have the connotation of primitive, individualistic markings but carries instead the new rhythm of mechanization, for the masses appear with their regularity and patterns of bodies as ornaments. I would suggest, however, that the mechanical and the primitive are far from mutually exclusive categories. Even in the brief passage just quoted, one cannot help but notice that this song of modern mechanization beats to a jungle beat ("Tapping their feet in fast tempo") and that the "conveyor belt" resembles an "undulating snake."

31. Lepecki goes on to argue that "the centrality of the racialized Other [provided] a source for choreographic mobility" (*Exhausting Dance*, 18). This important point will be further developed by Jayna Brown when she contends that the black woman's body in motion was "central to the anxieties and hopes embedded in white ideas of the modern city space" (Brown, *Babylon Girls*, 2). This discussion contributes to this line of inquiry by uncovering the literal and philosophic intersections between Baker in particular and the architects who were crucial figures in the making and imagining of the modern city and building.

32. Rose, *Jazz Cleopatra*, 24.

33. Colquhoun, *Modern Architecture*, 62–64. The Tessenow and Dalcroze collaboration also points to a larger set of issues, which are beyond the scope of this project, about ideals of bodily discipline and German nationalism. See Ferlenga, "From Hellerau to the Bauhuas."

34. Émile Jaques-Dalcroze (1865–1950) was fascinated by the so-called irregular rhythms of Arabic music and its "natural" and kinesthetic relations to the body. Thus, on the Tessenow-Appia stage, the performance taking place onstage harks back to Primitivist and Orientalist notions of body and rhythm that weaved seamlessly into neoclassical principles of modern harmony. For an introduction to the Tessenow and Dalcroze collaboration and German nationalism, see Ferlenga, "From Hellerau to the Bauhuas." For Jaques-Dalcroze's interest in Arabic music, see Jaques-Dalcroze, *The Jaques-Dalcroze Method*. The particular performance in the image cited in the body of my text most probably came from one of Jaques-Dalcroze's "eurythmic" performances and possibly even the most famous one, called *Orfeo*, performed in 1912 and often seen as the culmination of the Dalcroze method.

35. We might think, too, of Ruth St. Denis and her student Martha Graham, who have openly acknowledged their "Oriental" influences.

36. Brown, *Babylon Girls*; Brooks, "The End of the Line."

37. Haraway reimagines what she calls a "postmodern feminism" by suggesting that "Modern medicine is also full of cyborgs, of couplings between organism and machine, each conceived as coded devices, in an intimacy and with a power that was not generated in the history of sexuality. Cyborg 'sex' restores some of the lovely replicative baroque of ferns and invertebrates (such nice organic prophylactics against heterosexism). Cyborg replication is uncoupled from organic reproduction. Modern production seems like a dream of cyborg colonization work, a dream that makes the nightmare of Taylorism seem idyllic" (Haraway, "A Cyborg Manifesto," 151).

38. This discussion about Baker as Raggedy Ann is wholly indebted to Susan Stewart's insights into this image in the course of our discussions about Baker.

Chapter 8

1. Rose, *Jazz Cleopatra*.
2. Shakespeare, *The Merchant of Venice*; all quotes from Act III, scene 2.

3. It is beyond the scope of this project, but we should note that the nexus of issues that I am raising about race, gender, and surface/aesthetics has its haunting incarnations in American literature, too: from Edith Wharton (where the white female body becomes ornamentation itself; think *The House of Mirth*'s Lily Bart in her tableau vivant) to Maxine Hong Kingston (where social inscriptions get literally written on the body in *The Woman Warrior*) to Toni Morrion's fraught meditation on racialized beauty in *The Bluest Eye* to Ntozake Shange's reincarnation of the Baker-Cleopatra figure in *For Colored Girls Who Have Considered Suicide When the Rainbow Is Enuf*. One might suggest that all these texts are critically engaged with the historic tradition of enlisting feminine and racialized surfaces as aesthetic categories.

4. Freud, "The Theme of the Three Caskets" (1913), *SE*, 12:291.

5. Freud, "The Theme of the Three Caskets," 299.

6. Freud, "The Theme of the Three Caskets," 292.

7. Freud, "The Theme of the Three Caskets," 294.

8. Freud, "Anxiety and Instinctual Life" (1932), *SE*, 81–111; emphasis in original.

9. Freud, "Anxiety and Instinctual Life," 101

10. Leader, *Stealing the Mona Lisa*, 84.

11. The connections among femininity, waste, and racial exoticism can also be found in other incarnations in Le Corbusier's writings. In his infamous war against color, we find simultaneously an ardent indulgence in the senses of colors: "What shimmering silks, what fancy, glittery marbles, what opulent bronzes and golds! What fashionable blacks, what striking vermilions, what silver lamé, from Byzantium and the orient! Enough. Such stuff founders in a narcotic haze. Let's have done with it. . . . It is time to crusade for whiteness and Diogenes" (Le Corbusier, *The Decorative Art of Today*, 135). As is obvious by now, this "crusade" to debunk social values involves highly complex negotiations with (racialized and feminized) sartorial splendor.

12. Tanizaki, *In Praise of Shadows*, 6–7.

13. Freud, *Civilization and Its Discontents* (1919–1920), *SE*, 21:64.

14. McClintock, *Imperial Leather*, 207–231.

15. Le Corbusier, *The Decorative Art of Today*, 188.

16. Loos, *Spoken into the Void*, 49.

17. Foster, *Prosthetic Gods*.

18. Loos, *Spoken into the Void*, 46, 49.

19. Le Corbusier, *The Decorative Art of Today*, 190. There remains much to be done on the topic of Le Corbusier's relationship to colors. He

is known for his denigration of colors, but his early work was deeply engaged with so-called exotic colors. From his first book, *Journey to the East*, to his later works, Le Corbusier repeatedly acknowledged the primitive nostalgia behind the futuristic idea of "a coat of white paint": "Whitewash has been associated with human habitation since the birth of mankind" (*The Decorative Art of Today*, 190). His dreams of the future thus express longings for a prehistory at once primitivized and racialized.

20. Le Corbusier calls both images absolute examples of what he refers to as "x-ray" (*The Decorative Art of Today*, 190) beauty. As a modern invention that uses the contrast between light and dark to reveal what was previously invisible to the eye, the X-ray promises to penetrate opaque surfaces and reveal "inner truths." (Is the white of Ripolin transparency or opacity?) The thick coat of Ripolin is thus not free from a longing for transparency, one that is predicated on the balanced interplay between light and shadow, between a fantasized past and an imagined future. Moreover, as if in anxious repudiation of the charge of nationalistic arrogance, Le Corbusier will insist on the democracy rather than imperialism of "whitewashing": "whitewash is the wealth of the poor and of the rich—of everybody, just as bread, milk and water are the wealth of the slave and of the king" (*The Decorative Art of Today*, 192).

21. Tanizaki, *In Praise of Shadows*, 48–49.

22. Tanizaki, *In Praise of Shadows*, 63–64; my emphasis.

23. See Morrison, *Playing in the Dark*.

24. For an intriguing meditation by Tanizaki on the intimate connection between tattoos and (dirty/marked) perverse femininity, see "The Tattooer" ("Shisei," 1910), in Tanizaki, *Seven Japanese Tales*, 160–169.

25. Afong Moy was brought to the United States by Nathaniel and Frederick Carne (the Carne Brothers) as an "exotic oddity." She was thought to have toured the United States between 1834 and 1847. In 1850, a woman named Pwan-ye-koo was part of P. T. Barnum's "Chinese family" exhibit. These kinds of exhibitions clearly partook of the ethnographic displays employed by world's fairs at the turn of the century, as well as the "freak show" tradition. See Tchen, *New York before Chinatown*, 97–130; Ling, *Surviving on the Gold Mountain*, 1–3; Moon, *Yellowface*, 63; Barnum and Whalen, *The Life of P. T. Barnum*, 347; see also the Barnum and Bailey Collection at Princeton University's Firestone Library.

26. Hartman, *Lose Your Mother*, 47.

27. The critique of civilization that we are tracking is repeatedly suggested by the film but equally carefully rejected by the plot, which ultimately aims to

displace that very critique. Hence the specter of Max's own undisciplined and potentially soiled body gets displaced onto his promiscuous wife, just as the problem of French smells gets displaced onto primitive manure. But if Max's highly jeopardized subjectivity is preserved by the film—not least in the ending where everything turns out to be his harmless daydream—our viewing subjectivity is not.

28. Beller, *The Cinematic Mode of Production*, 9.
29. Groo, "Mysterious Unkillable Something."
30. Magriel, *Chronicles of the American Dance*, and De Mille, *The Book of the Dance*, explore how native American black dance and music always itself presents a record of the interchange between blacks and whites rather than a pure form.
31. Pietz, "The Problem of the Fetish."
32. On the connection between the idea of purity and modernity, see Wigley, *White Walls, Designer Dresses*, especially 3–12. On cleanliness and imperialism, see McClintock, *Imperial Leather*, especially 203–231.

Chapter 9

1. Cheng, *The Melancholy of Race*.
2. See Jay, *Downcast Eyes*. The visual culture that accompanies the Euro-American racial imaginary—from early ethnographic representations (expositions, "freak" shows, daguerreotypes, postcards, paintings, photography, and documentaries) to the more explicitly eroticized racial staging in contemporary culture (video games, pornography, and so forth)—offers overwhelming evidence for this reading.
3. See Gilroy, *The Black Atlantic*; Lewis, *A Power Stronger Than Itself*; Moten, *In the Break*; Weheliye, *Phonographies*. The suspicion of the visual and the visible is also why the trope of invisibility, from Ralph Ellison's *Invisible Man* to Toni Morrison's *The Bluest Eye*, is often taken to signal the repercussions of racial blindness rather than more fraught meditations on the interdependence of social (in)visibility.
4. Yoshino, *Covering*.
5. Harris, "Whiteness as Property," 278.
6. Yoshino, *Covering*, 117.
7. Yoshino, *Covering*, 11.
8. Yoshino, *Covering*, 11.

Chapter 10

1. De Rudbeck, "Une demi-heure intime"; quoted by Lemke, *Primitivist Modernism*, 111.

2. This is a coy response on many levels, not the least of which is the fact that Baker most certainly would have been familiar with who Pablo Picasso was. Not only do her biographers Lynn Haney and Jean-Claude Baker, her adopted son, claim that she sat for and had an affair with him, but we also know that Baker moved among the social and artistic elites of Paris. See Haney, *Naked at the Feast*, 63, 67, 70, 199; Baker and Chase, *Josephine Baker*, 421.

Works Cited

Abatino, Pepito. *Josephine Baker vue par la presse française*. Paris: Les Editions Isis, 1931.

Agamben, Giorgio. *Homo Sacer: Soveriegn Power and Bare Life*. Translated by Daniel Heller-Roazen. Stanford, CA: Stanford University Press, 1998.

Altman, Matthew C. "Freud among the Ruins: Revisions of Psychoanalytic Method." Paper presented at the Society for Philosophy in the Contemporary World Conference, Estes Park, CO, 1999.

Anzieu, Didier. "L'enveloppe sonore du soi." *Nouvelle Revue de Psychanalyse* 13 (1976): 161–179.

Anzieu, Didier. *The Skin Ego*. Translated by Chris Turner. New Haven, CT: Yale University Press, 1989.

Bacon, Mardges. *Le Corbusier in America*. Cambridge, MA: MIT Press, 2001.

Baker, Jean-Claude, and Chris Chase. *Josephine Baker: The Hungry Heart*. New York: First Cooper Square Press, 2001.

Baker, Josephine. *The Rainbow Children*. Amsterdam: Mulder & Zoon, 1958.

Banta, Martha. *Taylored Lives: Narrative Productions in the Age of Taylor, Veblen, and Ford*. Chicago: University of Chicago Press, 1995.

Barnum, Phineas Taylor, and Terence Whalen. *The Life of P. T. Barnum*. New York: Cosimo, 1855/2006.

Barrucand, Marianne, and Achim Bednorz. *Moorish Architecture in Andalusia*. Cologne: Taschen, 2007.

Barthes, Roland. *Mythologies*. Translated by Annette Lavers. New York: Hill & Wang, 1972.

Beller, Jonathan. *The Cinematic Mode of Production: Attention Economy and the Society of the Spectacle*. Hanover, NH: Dartmouth University Press, 2006.

Benthien, Claudia. *Skin: On the Cultural Border between Self and the World*. New York: Columbia University Press, 1965.

Bentley, Toni. *Sisters of Salome*. New York: Bison, 2005.

Berger, John. *Ways of Seeing*. New York: Penguin, 1927.

Berman, Illa. "Civilized Planes, Sexual Surfaces, Savage Territories." *Appendix: Culture, Theory. Praxis* 4 (1999): 7–27.

Berman, Marshall. *All That Is Solid Melts into Air: The Experience of Modernity*. New York: Simon & Schuster, 1982.

Bhabha, Homi K. *The Location of Culture*. New York: Routledge, 1994.

Blanchard, Pascal, Eric Deroo, and Gilles Manceron, eds. *Le Paris noir*. Paris: Hazan, 2001.

Borshuk, Michael. "An Intelligence of the Body: Disruptive Parody through Dance in the Early Performances of Josephine Baker." In *EmBODYing Liberation: The Black Body in American Dance*, edited by Dorothea Fischer-Hornung and Alison D. Goeller, 41–58. Münster: Literature, 2001.

Brooks, Daphne A. "The End of the Line: Josephine Baker and the Politics of Black Women's Corporeal Comedy." Paper presented at the Baker Centennial Conference at Barnard College, New York, 2006. *S & F Online* 6.1–6.2 (Fall 2007/Spring 2008). https://sfonline.barnard.edu/the-end-of-the-linejosephine-baker-and-the-politics-of-black-womens-corporeal-comedy/.

Brown, Bill. *A Sense of Things: The Object Matter of American Literature*. Chicago: University of Chicago Press, 2003.

Brown, Jayna. *Babylon Girls: Black Women Performers and the Shaping of the Modern*. Durham, NC: Duke University Press, 2008.

Brown, Judith. *Glamour in Six Dimensions: Modernism, Aesthetics, Culture*. Ithaca, NY: Cornell University Press, 2009.

Burns, Karen. "A House for Josephine Baker." In *Postcolonial Space(s)*, edited by G. B. Nalbantoglu and C. T. Wong Thai, 53–72. New York: Princeton Architectural Press, 1997.

Butler, Judith. *Bodies That Matter: On the Discursive Limits of "Sex."* New York: Routledge, 1993.

Chapman, Peter. *Bananas! How the United Fruit Company Changed the World*. New York: Canongate, 2008.

Cheng, Anne Anlin. *The Melancholy of Race: Psychoanalysis, Assimilation, and Hidden Grief*. New York: Oxford University Press, 2001.

Clifton, Lara, Sarah Ainslie, and Julie Cook, eds. *Baby Oil and Ice: Striptease in East London*. London: Do-Not Press, 2005.

Coffman, Elizabeth Ann. "Uncanny Performances in Colonial Narratives: Josephine Baker in *Princess Tam Tam*." *Paradoxa: Studies in World Literary Genres* 3, nos. 3–4 (1997): 379–394.

Colomina, Beatriz. *Privacy and Publicity: Modern Architecture as Mass Media*. Cambridge, MA: MIT Press, 1996.

Colomina, Beatriz. "The Split Wall: Domestic Voyeurism." In *Sexuality and Space*, edited by B. Colomina, 73–128. New York: Princeton Architectural Press, 1992.

Colquhoun, Alan. *Modern Architecture*. New York: Oxford University Press, 2002.

Connor, Steven. *The Book of Skin*. London: Reaktion Books, 2004.

Cummings, E. E. "Vive la Folie!" *Vanity Fair*, September 1926, 55, 116.

Cunard, Nancy, ed. *Negro: An Anthology*. New York: Negro University Press, 1934.

Dalton, Karen, and Henry Louis Gates Jr. "Josephine Baker and Paul Colin: African American Dance Seen through Parisian Eyes." *Critical Inquiry* 24 (1998): 903–934. [Reprinted as the introduction to *Josephine Baker and La Revue Nègre: Paul Colin's Lithographs of Le Tumulte Noir in Paris, 1927*. New York: Abrams, 1998.]

Daly, Nicholas. "That Obscure Object of Desire: Victorian Commodity Culture and the Fictions of the Mummy." *Novel* 28, no. 1 (Autumn 1994): 24–51.

Davis, Diane. "Signifyin' Josephine." *Appendix: Culture, Theory, Praxis* 4 (1999): 28–45.

De Mille, Agnes. *The Book of the Dance*. New York: Golden Press, 1961.

De Rudbeck, I. "Une demi-heure intime avec Joséphine Baker et sa panthere 'Chiquita.'" *Marseille Matin*, September 20, 1933.

Doane, Mary Ann. *Femmes Fatales: Feminism, Film Theory, Psychoanalysis*. New York: Routledge, 1991.

Doane, Mary Ann. "The Voice in the Cinema: The Articulation of Body and Space." *Yale French Studies* 61 (1980): 33–50.

Douglas, Ann. *Terrible Honesty: Mongrel Manhattan in the 1920s*. New York: Farrar, Straus and Giroux, 1995.

Dyer, Richard. *Heavenly Bodies: Film Stars and Society*. New York: St. Martin's Press, 1986.

Dyer, Richard. *White*. New York: Routledge, 1997.

Edwards, Brent Hayes. *The Practice of Diaspora: Literature, Translation, and the Rise of Black Internationalism*. Cambridge, MA: Harvard University Press, 2003.

El-Dahdah, Farès. "The Josephine Baker House: For Loos's Pleasure." *Assemblage* 26 (1995): 72–87.

Eleb-Vidal, Monique. "Hotel Particuliére." In *Le Corbusier, une encyclopédie*, edited by J. Lucan, 174–176. Paris: Centre Georges Pompidou, 1987.

Eze, Emmanuel Chukudi, ed. *Race and the Enlightenment: A Reader*. Cambridge, MA: Blackwell, 1997.

Faber, Monika, ed. *D'Ora: Vienna and Paris, 1907–1957: The Photography of Dora Kallmus*. Poughkeepsie, NY: Vassar Art Gallery, 1987.

Fanon, Frantz. *Black Skin, White Masks*. Translated by Charles Markmann. New York: Grove Press, 1967.

Fend, Mechthild. "Bodily and Pictiral Surafces: Skin in French Art and Medicine, 1790–1860." *Art History* 28, no. 3 (June 2005): 311–339.

Ferlenga, Alberto. "From Hellerau to the Bauhuas: Memory and Modernity of the German Garden City." *The New City* 3 (Fall 1996): 50–69.

Flanner, Janet. *Paris Was Yesterday, 1925–1939*. New York: Viking, 1972.

Fleissner, Jennifer L. *Woman, Compulsion, Modernity*. Chicago: University of Chicago Press, 2004.

Fletcher, Richard. *Moorish Spain*. Berkeley: University of California Press, 2006.

Foster, Hal. "The Art of Fetishism: Notes on Dutch Still Life." In *Fetishism as Cultural Discourse*, edited by Emily S. Apter and William Pietz, 251–265. Ithaca, NY: Cornell University Press, 1993.

Foster, Hal. "The Primitive Unconscious of Modern Art." *October* 34 (Autumn 1985): 45–70.

Foster, Hal. *Prosthetic Gods*. Cambridge, MA: MIT Press, 2006.

"French Visitor Here Urges 'Garden-Cities' Up in the Air." *Philadelphia Inquirer*, November 9, 1935, 2.

Freud, Sigmund. *The Standard Edition of the Complete Psychological Works of Sigmund Freud (SE in text)*. Translated by James Strachey. London: Hogarth Press, 1955.

Fry, Roger. "The Art of the Bushman (1910)." In Roger Fry, *Vision and Design*. London: Chatto & Windus, 56–64. 1920.

Fry, Roger. "Negro Sculpture (1920)." In Roger Fry, *Vision and Design*, 65–69. London: Chatto & Windus, 1920.

Gaines, Jane. "Costume and Narrative: How Dress Tells the Woman's Story." In *Fabrications: Costume and the Female Body*, edited by Jane Gaines and Charlotte Herzog, 180–211. New York: Routledge, 1990.

Garber, Marjorie B. *Vested Interests: Cross-Dressing and Cultural Anxiety*. New York: Routledge, 1997.

Garelick, Rhonda K. *Electric Salome: Loie Fuller's Performance of Modernism*. Princeton, NJ: Princeton University Press, 2007.

Gilman, Sander L. *Difference and Pathology: Stereotypes of Sexuality, Race, and Madness*. Ithaca, NY: Cornell University Press, 1985.

Gilot, Françoise, and Carlton Lake. *Life with Picasso*. New York: McGraw Hill, 1964.

Gilroy, Paul. *The Black Atlantic: Modernity and Double Consciousness*. Cambridge, MA: Harvard University Press, 1993.

Glover, Kaiama L. "Postmodern Homegirl." *New York Times*, June 3, 2007. https://www.nytimes.com/2007/06/03/books/review/Glover-t.html?searchResultPosition=1.

Goffe, Leslie Gordon. *When Banana Was King: The Life and Times of Jamaican "Banana King" Alfred Constantine Goffe*. Kingston, Jamaica: LMH, 2006.

Goldsmith, K., W. Kostenbaum, and R. Wolf, eds. *I'll Be Your Mirror: The Selected Andy Warhol Interviews, 1962–1987*. New York: Carroll and Graft, 2004.

Groenendijk, Paul, and Piet Vollaard. *Adolf Loos, Huis voor Josephine Baker (Adolf Loos, House for Josephine Baker)*. Rotterdam: Uitgeverij 010, 1985.

Groo, Katharine. "Mysterious Unkillable Something: Rereading Josephine Baker and the Surface of Ethnographic Cinema." Paper presented at the Rethinking the Surface Conference at Cornell University, Ithaca, NY, 2006.

Habel, Ylza. "To Stockholm with Love: The Critical Reception of Josephine Baker, 1927–1935." *Film History: An Interdisciplinary Journal* 17 (2005): 125–138.

Haney, Lynn. *Naked at the Feast: A Biography of Josephine Baker*. New York: Dodd, Mead, 1981.

Hardy, Thomas. *Tess of the d'Urvervilles*. New York: Penguin, 2003.

Haraway, Donna. "A Cyborg Manifesto: Science, Technology, and Socialist-Feminism in the Late Twentieth Century." In Donna Haraway, *Simians, Cyborgs and Women: The Reinvention of Nature*, 149–181. New York: Routledge, 1991.

Harris, Cheryl I. "Whiteness as Property." In *Critical Race Theory: The Key Writings That Formed the Movement*, edited by Kimberlé Crenshaw, Neil Gotanda, Gary Peller, and Kendall Thomas, 276–277. New York: New Press, 1995.

Hartman, Saidiya V. *Lose Your Mother: A Journey along the Atlantic Slave Route*. New York: Farrar, Straus and Giroux, 2007.

Henderson, Mae. "Josephine Baker and La Revue Nègre: From Ethnography to Performance." *Text and Performance Quarterly* 23 (2003): 107–133.

Henderson, Susan R. "Bachelor Culture in the Work of Adolf Loos." *Journal of Architectural Education* 55 (2002): 125–135.

Herrmann, Wolfgang. *Gottfried Semper: In Search of Architecture*. Cambridge, MA: MIT Press, 1984.

hooks, bell. *Black Looks: Race and Representation*. Toronto: Between the Lines, 1992.

Huysmans, Joris-Karl. *Against Nature*. Translated by Robert Baldick. New York: Penguin, 2004.

Jaques-Dalcroze, Émile. *The Jaques-Dalcroze Method of Eurythmics*. London: Archival Reprint, 1920.

Jay, Martin. *Downcast Eyes: The Denigration of Vision in Twentieth Century French Thought*. Berkeley: University of California Press, 1994.

Jordy, William H. "Masonry Block and Metal Skeleton." *American Buildings and Their Architects*, Vol. 4: *Progressive and Academic Ideals at the Turn of the Twentieth Century*, 28–52. New York: Anchor Books, 1972.

Jules-Rosette, Bennetta. *Black Paris: The African Writer's Landscape*. Chicago: University of Illinois Press, 2000.

Jules-Rosette, Bennetta. *Josephine Baker in Art and Life: The Image and the Icon*. Urbana: University of Illinois Press, 2007.

Kenner, Hugh. *The Mechanic Muse*. New York: Oxford University Press, 1988.

Khanna, Ranjana. *Dark Continents: Psychoanalysis and Colonialism*. Durham, NC: Duke University Press, 2003.

Knowles, Eric. *Miller's 100 Years of the Decorative Arts: Victoriana, Arts and Crafts, Art Nouveau, and Art Deco*. London: Mitchell Beazley, 1998.

Koeppel, Dan. *Banana: The Fate of the Fruit That Changed the World*. New York: Hudson Street Press, 2007.

Kracauer, Siegfried. "Girls and Crisis." In *The Weimar Republic Sourcebook*, edited by Anton Kaes, Martin Jay, and Edward Dimenberg, 565–566. Berkeley: University of California Press, 1995.

Krauss, Rosalind. "Preying on 'Primitivism.'" *Art and Text* 17 (1985): 11–62.

Laplanche, Jean. *Life and Death in Psychoanalysis*. Translated by Jeffrey Mehlman. Baltimore: Johns Hopkins University Press, 1985.

Laplanche, Jean, and J. B. Pontalis. "Fantasy and the Origins of Sexuality." In *Formations of Fantasy*, edited by Victor Burgin, 5–29. New York: Routledge, 1986.

Leader, Darian. *Stealing the Mona Lisa: What Art Stops Us from Seeing*. Washington, DC: Shoemaker and Hoard, 2002.

Le Corbusier. *The Decorative Art of Today (L'art décoratif d'aujourd'hui)*. Translated by James I. Dunnett. Cambridge, MA: MIT Press, 1987.

Le Corbusier. *Journey to the East (Le voyage d'orient)*. Translated by Ivan Zaknic. Cambridge, MA: MIT Press, 2007.

Le Corbusier. *Oeuvre Complète, 1910–1929*. Edited by Willy Boesinger. Paris: Artemis-Aidc, 1992.

Le Corbusier. *Precisions: On the Present State of Architecture and City Planning*. Translated by Edith Schreiber Aujame. Cambridge, MA: MIT Press, 1991.

Le Corbusier. *When the Cathedrals Were White*. Translated by Francis E. Hyslop Jr. New York: McGraw Hill, 1947.

Lemke, Sieglinde. *Primitivist Modernism: Black Culture and the Origins of Transatlantic Modernism*. New York: Oxford University Press, 1998.

Lepecki, Andre. *Exhausting Dance: Performance and the Politics of Movement*. New York: Routledge, 2006.

Lewis, George. *A Power Stronger Than Itself: The AACM and American Experimental Music*. Chicago: University of Chicago Press, 2008.

Ling, Huping. *Surviving on the Gold Mountain: A History of Chinese American Women and Their Lives*. Albany: State University of New York Press, 1998.

Lombroso, Cesare. *Criminal Man*. Translated by Mary Gibson and Nicole Hahn. New York: Putnam, 1911.

Loos, Adolf. "Ornament and Crime." In *The Architecture of Adolf Loos: An Arts Council Exhibition*, edited by Yehuda Safran and Wilfried Wang. London: Arts Council, 1985. 100–103.

Loos, Adolf. "The Principle of Cladding." *Spoken into the Void: Collected Essays 1897–1900*. Trans. Jane O. Newman and John H. Smith. Cambridge, MA: MIT Press, 1982. 66–67.

Loos, Adolf. *Spoken into the Void: Collected Essays 1897–1900*. Translated by Jane O. Newman and John H. Smith. Cambridge, MA: MIT Press, 1982.

Magriel, Paul David, ed. *Chronicles of the American Dance*. New York: Da Capo, 1978.

Malraux, André. *Picasso's Mask*. Translated by June Guichardnaud and Gauchos Guichardnaud. New York: Holt, Rinehart and Winston, 1976. (The original, *La tête d'obsidienne*, Paris: Gallimard, appeared in 1974.)

McCarren, Felicia. "The Use-Value of 'Josephine Baker.'" Paper presented at the Baker Centennial Conference at Barnard College, New York, 2006. *S &*

F Online 6.1–6.2 (Fall 2007/Spring 2008). https://sfonline.barnard.edu/the-use-value-of-josephine-baker/.

McClintock, Anne. *Imperial Leather: Race, Gender, and Sexuality in the Colonial Contest*. New York: Routledge, 1995.

McLeod, Mary, ed. *Charlotte Perriand: An Art of Living*. New York: H. N. Abrams, 2003.

Meikle, Jeffrey L. *American Plastic: A Cultural History*. New Brunswick, NJ: Rutgers University Press, 1997.

Moberg, Mark, Steve Striffler, Lura Reynolds, and John Suluri, eds. *Banana Wars: Power, Production, and the Trade in the Americas*. Durham, NC: Duke University Press, 2003.

Moon, Kyrstyn R. *Yellowface: Creating the Chinese in American Popular Music and Performance, 1850–1920s*. New Brunswick, NJ: Rutgers University Press, 2004.

Morrison, Toni. *The Bluest Eye*. New York: Plume, 1970.

Morrison, Toni. *Playing in the Dark: Whiteness and the Literary Imagination*. Cambridge, MA: Harvard University Press, 1992.

Moten, Fred. *In the Break: The Aesthetics of the Black Radical Tradition*. Minneapolis: University of Minnesota Press, 2003.

Mullen, Harryette. *Trimmings*. New York: Tender Buttons, 1991.

Münz, Ludwig, and Gustav Künstler. *Adolf Loos, Pioneer of Modern Architecture*. Translated by Harold Meek. London: Thames & Hudson, 1966.

Ngai, Sianne. "Black Venus, Blonde Venus." In *Bad Modernisms*, edited by Douglas Mao and Rebecca L. Walkowitz, 145–178. Durham, NC: Duke University Press, 2006.

Pacteau, Francette. *The Symptom of Beauty*. Cambridge, MA: Harvard University Press, 1994.

Parks, Suzan-Lori. "The Rear End Exists." *Women: A Cultural Review* 5, no. 2 (Autumn 1994): 11–17.

Pietz, William. "The Problem of the Fetish." *Res: Journal of Anthropology and Aesthetics* 9 (1988): 110–122.

Pratt, John Clark. *Punishment and Civilization: Penal Tolerance and Intolerance in Modern Society*. Thousand Oaks, CA: Sage, 2002.

Quetglas i Riusech, José. "Lo placentero." *Carrer de la Ciutat* 9–10 (January 1980): 2.

Robinson, Susan. "Josephine Baker." *Gibbs Magazine*, August 1, 2005. http://www.gibbsmagazine.com/Josephine%20Baker.htm. Retrieved January 2010.

Rose, Phyllis. *Jazz Cleopatra: Josephine Baker in Her Time*. New York: Vintage, 1989.

Rosolato, Guy. "La voix: Entre corps et langage." *Revue Française de Psychanalyse* 37, no. 1 (1974): 75–94.

Rowe, Colin, and Robert Slutzky. "Transparency: Literal and Phenomenal." *Perspecta*, no. 8 (1963): 45–54.

Rubin, William. *Primitivism in 20th Century Art: Affinity of the Tribal and the Modern*. New York: Harry N. Abrams, 1998.

WORKS CITED

Rykwert, Joseph. "Adolf Loos: The New Vision." In Joseph Rykwert, *The Necessity of Artifice*, 67–73. New York: Rizzoli, 1982.

Samuel, Flora. *Le Corbusier: Architect and Feminist*. West Essex: John Wiley, 2004.

Sauvage, Marcel. *Les mémoires de Joséphine Baker*. Paris: Éditions Kra, 1927.

Scheper, Jeanne. "'Of La Baker, I Am a Disciple': The Diva Politics of Reception." *Camera Obscura* 65 (2007): 73–101.

Schor, Naomi. *Reading in Detail: Aesthetics and the Feminine*. New York: Routledge, 2006.

Sekula, Allan. "The Body and the Archive." *October* 39 (Winter 1986): 3–64.

Seltzer, Mark. *Bodies and Machines*. New York: Routledge, 1972.

Semper, Gottfried. *The Four Elements of Architecture and Other Writings*. Translated by Harry Francis Mallgrave and Wolfgang Herrmann. Cambridge: Cambridge University Press, 1989.

Seshadri-Crooks, Kalpana. *Desiring Whiteness: A Lacanian Analysis of Race*. New York: Routledge, 2000.

Shakespeare, William. *The Merchant of Venice*. In *The Complete Signet Classic Shakespeare*, 607–637. New York: Harcourt Brace Jovanovich, 1972.

Shapira, Elana. "Dressing a Celebrity: Adolf Loos's House for Josephine Baker." *Studies in the Decorative Arts* 11, no. 2 (Spring–Summer 2004): 2–20.

Sharpley-Whiting, T. Denean. *Black Venus: Sexualized Savages, Primal Fears, and Primitive Narratives in French*. Durham, NC: Duke University Press, 1999.

Shteir, Rachel. *Striptease: The Untold History of the Girlie Show*. New York: Oxford University Press, 2005.

Sigel, Lisa Z. *Governing Pleasures: Pornography and Social Change in England, 1815–1914*. New Brunswick, NJ: Rutgers University Press, 2002.

Silverman, Kaja. *The Acoustic Mirror: Female Voice in Psychoanalysis and Cinema*. Bloomington: Indiana University Press, 1988.

Simmel, Georg. "The Metropolis and Mental Life (1903)." In Geog Simmel, *The Sociology of Georg Simmel*, translated by Kurt Wolff, 409–424. New York: Free Press, 1950.

Spillers, Hortense J. "Mama's Baby, Papa's Maybe: An American Grammar Book." In *The Black Feminist Reader*, edited by Joy James and T. Denean Sharpley-Whiting, 57–87. Boston: Wiley-Blackwell, 2000.

Stovall, Tyler Edward, ed. *Paris Noir: African Americans in the City of Light*. Boston: Houghton Mifflin, 1996.

Stuart, Andrea. "Looking at Josephine Baker." *Women: A Cultural Review* 5, no. 2 (1994): 137–143.

Tanizaki, Junichiro. *In Praise of Shadows*. Translated by Thomas Harper and Edward Seidensticker. New York: Vintage, 2001.

Tanizaki, Junichiro. *Seven Japanese Tales*. Translated by Howard Hibbett. New York: Vintage, 1996.

Tanzer, Kim. "Baker's Loos and Loos's Loss: Architecting the Body." *Center: A Journal for Architecture in America* 9 (1995): 76–89.

Tchen, John Kuo Wei. *New York before Chinatown*. Baltimore: Johns Hopkins University Press, 2001.

Thompson, Krista. "The Sound of Light: Reflections on Art History in the Visual Culture of Hip Hop." *Art Bulletin* 41, no. 4 (December 2009): 481–505.

Tichy, Marina, and Sylvia Zwettler-Otte. *Freud in der Presse: Rezeption Sigmund Freuds und der Psychoanalyse in Österreich 1895–1938*. Vienna: Sonderzahl, 1999.

Torgovnick, Marianna. *Gone Primitive: Savage Intellects, Modern Lives*. Urbana: University of Illinois Press, 1990.

Tournikiotis, Panayotis. *Adolf Loos*. Translated by Marguerite McGoldrick. New York: Princeton Architectural Press, 1994.

Wallace, Irving, and David Wallechinsky, eds. *The People's Almanac*. Garden City, NY: Doubleday, 1975.

Walton, Jean. *Fair Sex, Savage Dreams: Race, Psychoanalysis, Sexual Difference*. Durham, NC: Duke University Press, 2001.

Ward, Philip M. "The Electric Body: Nancy Cunard Sees Josephine Baker." Paper presented in the Nancy Cunard Conference, Anglia Polytechnic University, Cambridge, 2001.

Weheliye, Alexander. *Phonographies: Grooves in Sonic Afro-Modernity*. Durham, NC: Duke University Press, 2005.

Welch, Barbara M. *Survival by Association: Supply Management Landscapes of the Eastern Caribbean*. Montreal: McGill-Queen's University Press, 1996.

Wigley, Mark. *White Walls, Designer Dresses: The Fashioning of Modern Architecture*. Cambridge, MA: MIT Press, 2001.

Wilde, Oscar. *The Picture of Dorian Grey*. New York: Modern Library, 1998.

Wood, Jon. "Introduction." In *Shine: Sculpture and Surface in the 1920s and 1930s*, 1–6. Exhibition catalogue, Leeds City Art Gallery, February 16–May 12, 2002. Leeds, UK: Henry Moore Institute, 2002.

Woolf, Virginia. "Modern Fiction." In *The Common Reader*, edited by Andrew McNeillie, 146–154. New York: Mariner Books, [1925] 1984..

Woolf, Virginia. "Mr. Bennett and Mrs. Brown." In *The Essays of Virginia Woolf*, Vol. 3: 1919–1924, edited by Andrew McNeillie, 384–389. San Diego: Harcourt Brace, 1989.

Wortley, Richard. *A Pictorial History of Striptease: One Hundred Years of Undressing to Music*. London: Treasury, 1976.

Yoshino, Kenji. *Covering: The Hidden Assault on Our Civil Rights*. New York: Random House, 2006.

Zizek, Slovoj. *Enjoy Your Symptom: Jacques Lacan in Hollywood and Out*. New York: Routledge, 2001.

Index

For the benefit of digital users, indexed terms that span two pages (e.g., 52–53) may, on occasion, appear on only one of those pages.

Page numbers in italics denote illustrations.

Figures are indicated by *f* following the page number.